# CAMPAIGNS OF 1862 AND 1863.

# CAMPAIGNS

OF

# 1862 AND 1863

ILLUSTRATING

# THE PRINCIPLES OF STRATEGY.

BY

EMIL SCHALK,
AUTHOR OF "SUMMARY OF THE ART OF WAR."

SECOND EDITION.

PHILADELPHIA:
J. B. LIPPINCOTT & CO.
1863.

# PREFACE.

---

Few years of military annals are so fertile in events as that which has just expired. Full of varied chances, the year 1862 ought to teach us a great lesson. It ought to remind us that "The great principles of war cannot be violated with impunity." It may be interesting as well as useful to investigate the causes, both of the great disasters which have befallen our armies, and of the successes which they have achieved.

By passing in review the different operations, and by discussing them from a strictly military stand-point, we may so perceive the errors of the past campaign as to be able to avoid similar ones in the campaigns to come. These reasons have induced me to write a military review of the campaign of 1862, and even to discuss operations which will probably take place in 1863.

Presumptuous as it may appear to undertake such a task, I am encouraged to do so by the remarkable manner in which events coincided with a similar discussion given by me, in a work entitled "SUMMARY OF THE ART OF WAR," and written at the end of 1861.

I discussed in that work operations which were afterward made by our generals. I pointed out the correct line of defense against these operations, and showed the results. The Rebels adopted this defense; the results were as I had shown they would be. The present work may therefore be considered as a kind of treatise on grand war, and as a sequel to my "Summary of the Art of War."

I hope the reader will judge it with indulgence, and, while perusing it, take into consideration that my only sources of information were the reports published in our newspapers, and such maps as may be found in any library.

E. S.

*January*, 1863.

# CONTENTS.

# CAMPAIGNS OF 1862 AND 1863.

---

THE discussion of events recently passed, and fresh in everybody's memory, is a difficult task, as impressions of all kinds are still alive, and passions on the subject are not entirely subdued. It is therefore necessary, before entering on the discussion of the past campaign, to establish a sound basis, or rather to give the reader a correct idea of what in war is to be considered right and what wrong.

For this, sound knowledge and thorough understanding of the great maxims of the art, and a familiar acquaintance with the great geographical features of the theater of the contest, are absolutely indispensable. We will, consequently, devote a few chapters to the principles of strategy, as applied to great wars of invasion; and we will consider the geography of the Southern Confederacy, in so far as it has an influence on military operations.

We hope that our readers will carefully peruse those chapters, though they may be somewhat dry, as the whole of the reasoning to come will be based upon, and will have reference to, what has been laid down in them.

# I.

## PRINCIPLES OF STRATEGY.

In order to understand the following pages, it is necessary to give a short exposition of the principal maxims of strategy. These maxims are deduced from the modes of operation in the field adopted by the great captains of all ages; they furnish the rules of action in offensive or defensive campaigns.

War has existed nearly since the creation of the world; the history of every country commences with war and the feats of its heroes. The objects for which war is waged have been in all ages nearly always the same. The principles on which it is conducted have remained unchanged from the first, although, with the progress of civilization, the understanding of those principles becomes more general, and the manner of fighting different.

The most complete discussion of the principles of strategy is to be found in Gen. Jomini's works, especially in his "Art of War." This work, though a standard one of its kind, is intended only for the military student, and requires considerable knowledge of military history before reading it. This is the reason why, instead of referring simply to his work, I present the following compact and easily understood treatise, which, however, will also be found in substance in my "*Summary of the Art of War.*"

Three great principles may be laid down as belonging to the entire science of war. They are—

1. To concentrate all disposable forces, and to act with the whole of them against a part only of the enemy's forces.

2. To act against the weakest part of the enemy; against his center if his forces be not united, and against his flank or rear, if they be concentrated. Also, to act against his communications without endangering our own.

3. Whatever plan of operations has been decided on, it should be executed with the utmost promptness, so that the object may be attained before the enemy can prevent it.

Simple as these three great maxims may appear, their application is nevertheless of the greatest difficulty. In fact, this application varies with every new tract of land upon which we enter; with every different position of the enemy, with every variation in the disposition of his forces and of our own army. In all these cases the circumstances vary, but the principles upon which to act remain the same; and it is in the right application of these maxims to circumstances that the qualities of a great commander are displayed.

Before going farther, let us give here a few definitions and explanations.

**Base of Operation.**—On opening a campaign we must have a line for the concentration of our troops, whereon to place our depots and magazines, and from which to advance to execute our different plans. This line is called the *base of operation.* The choice of this line is of the utmost importance, for the result of a whole campaign may depend upon it. Let *a b c d* be the theater of war. Now if *a c* and *a b* belong to us, and *b d* be the sea, or the frontier of some great neutral power, the army of the enemy has but

Fig. 1.

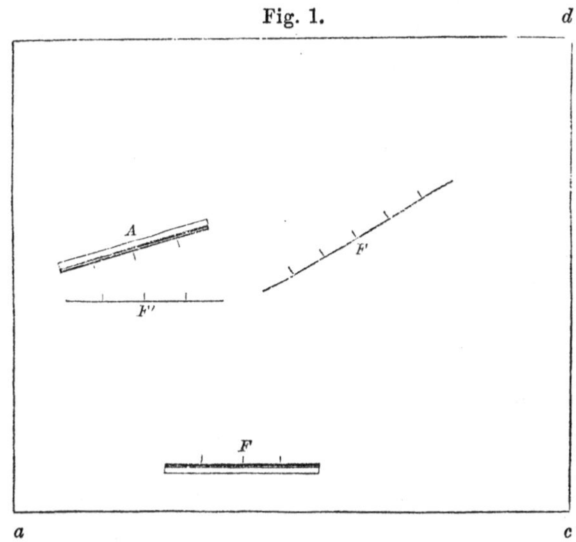


one line of retreat left, viz., *c d*. We may choose *a b* or *a c* for our base. In choosing *a b*, the enemy's army would always have its retreat to *c d* free; but in choosing *a c*, we may advance from *F* to *F′*, cut the army *A* from its communications, and force it into the corner *b*, where it would be obliged to surrender. The campaign of 1806 may serve as an illustration: *b d*, in this case, represents the North Sea; *a b* the Rhine, *a c* the Maine, and *c d* the Elbe; *c d* was the only retreat for the Prussian army *A*. The French army *F* advanced from *F* to *F′*, defeated the Prussian army *A* at

Jena, and threw it back on the North Sea, where the remnant of it surrendered.

Or if *a b* is our base, and *c d* that of the enemy, we might advance from *m* to *c* without fear of being driven from our communications, while the enemy would even be endangered by advancing on the straight line *m n*, because we would always be able to retreat to *a*; but the enemy having only a small base, will expose his own communications as soon as he tries to act on ours.

Fig. 2.

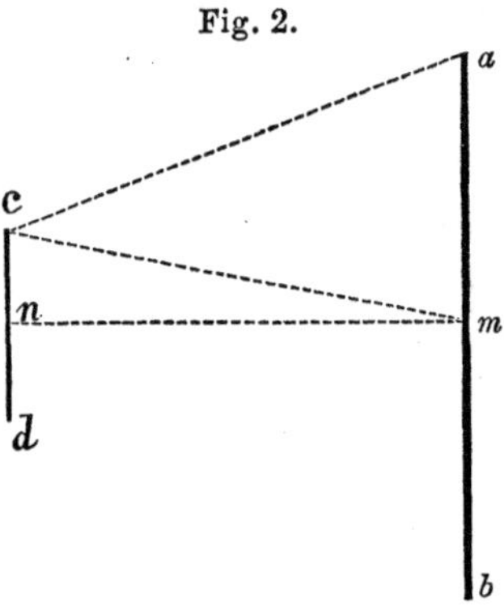


**Lines of Communication** are called the lines or roads joining us with our base, or to another army co-operating with us on the same theater of war.

**Lines of Operation.**—If the choice of the base of operation is of importance, that of the line of operation is still more so. We call line of operation the main road or direction which is followed by the principal body of the army. If there is but one army on the same frontier, the line will be simple; if there are two armies, there will be a double line of operation.

The interior line of operation is the line which two or more armies would follow, if attacked from different sides by different armies, but so that they would be enabled to unite before the various corps of the enemy could do so.

The way from *a* to *b*, in Fig. 3, would be the interior line; the way from *c* to *d*, the exterior line.

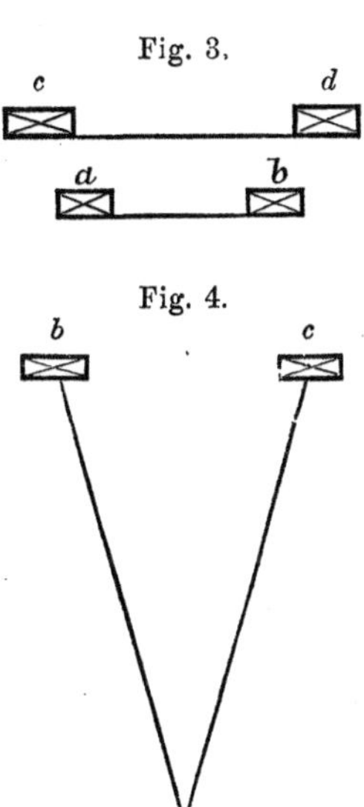

Fig. 3.
Fig. 4.

We call the lines of two or more armies or army corps, starting from distant points and meeting together in one, *concentric lines*. (See Fig. 4.) Divergent lines leave one point to arrive at two or three distant points. If leaving *a*, *a b* and *a c* are divergent lines; if *b* and *c*, they are concentric ones.

If an army is placed between two hostile armies, so that it can defeat either of them before they are able to effect a junction, its position is called a central one.

Besides the definitions already given, we call *strategic points and lines* all such points and lines on the theater of war the occupation of which may be of importance during the war.

We call *lines of defense* all those lines which we choose for defense, or which by the natural configuration of the ground admits of an easy defense. It is evident that the line must be a strategic one—that is, it must be so situated that by its occupation we prevent the enemy attaining his object.

Each theater of war can be divided into the three zones—right, left, and center.

As general maxims of strategy, we may enumerate the following:—

1. To turn to the best advantage the respective directions of our base of operation and that of the enemy.

2. To choose the one of the three zones of the theater of war on which we can cause the greatest disasters to the enemy with the least risk to ourselves.

3. In order to well direct the lines of operation in defense as well as in attack, the interior lines are always to be adopted. In defense, these lines ought to be concentric; in attack, which is just the reverse, they ought to be divergent.

4. No. 3 implies that we ought to choose our lines so that we can always unite our divisions before the enemy can unite his, and that with our united force we ought to beat him in detail.

5. To act with the utmost activity and speed.

It remains to be shown how these rules are to be applied to offensive and to defensive operations.

**Offensive Operations.**—Whatever be the geographical configuration of the theater of war, it can be divided into three zones—right, left, and center—as we have already seen; but a choice is to be made as to which of the three zones is to be the scene of operations.

Circumstances may be such that one, two, or even all three zones may be employed: in the first case, we should have a simple line; in the two others, several lines of operation.

1st. If there is but one line, two cases may occur—either that the enemy occupies a very extended line, or that he holds a concentrated position. In the first case, the most advantageous point to act on is the center, which we should break with our whole force, and then defeat each of the wings separately.

In 1796 Napoleon, when opposed to Beaulieu, whose line was extended from Genoa to Ceva, broke through the center of the Austro-Sardinian army at Montenotte, with his entire force, and then defeated the two wings, one after the other, in the engagements of Milesimo, Dego, and Mondovi.

In 1809, when opposed to the Archduke Charles, whose army also formed a very extended line, he acted in a similar way, and defeated successively the Austrian forces in the battles of Abensberg, Landshut, Eckmühl, and Ratisbon.

In the second case, if the enemy keep his forces concentrated, the manœuvre against his center is rendered impossible, or at least disadvantageous, and we should then see if an attack on one of the other two zones does not present the chance of our acting at once on the enemy's communications, without endangering our own.

Figures 1 and 2 will show how this is possible. When once on the enemy's communications, we cut off his line of retreat; to return to his base he is obliged to force his way with the bayonet; if he fails in this attempt and is defeated, he will be forced to surrender. Examples of such operations are to be found in the campaigns of 1800, 1805, and 1806. In 1805 Mack, with an Austrian army, near Ulm, was turned by Napoleon and obliged to capitulate. This result was obtained in consequence of the position and extension of the two bases of operation. Fig. 2 will explain this, by supposing that *a b* forms the base of the French, and that they advance from *a* to *n*, and that they cut the Austrian army, which has advanced in the direction of *m*, from its base *c d*. The case of the campaign of 1806 is explained under the head of base of operation, illustrating the meaning of Fig. 1.

Should the enemy, however, maintain such a position that neither the manœuvres against his center nor against his communications are possible, it will be necessary to resort to stratagems which shall induce him to make wrong movements, divide his troops, extend his lines, etc. For instance, we may give our whole army such a position, or we may, before the commencement of operations, place the several corps of our army in such a manner that they can act with the same facility against two or more points very distant from each other. The enemy is thus obliged to divide his force, and our first position must be chosen so that we may, by a few hidden and forced marches, unite our whole army on the decisive point; having carried which, we can then defeat the enemy in detail.

2d. If we form two lines of operation, we should follow divergent lines—that is, we should place our armies between those of the enemy, and transport our main body alternately from one army to the other. The enemy's armies being isolated, cannot unite, and must fall under the blows of our superior force.

The plan of the campaign of 1800, as devised by Napoleon, is the finest example of this that can be offered.

Melas, with a large army in Italy, had arrived at a short distance from the French frontier; Kray, with another army, threatened the Rhine. Moreau, near Basle, was to act against Kray, and the reserve army, disposed on the Swiss frontier, was to act in Italy. Napoleon's plan was for Moreau to pass through Switzerland, cross the Rhine at Shaffhausen, cut off Kray from his communications, and thereby destroy his army, while Napoleon himself crossed the Alps by the passes of the Great St. Bernard, Simplon, St. Gothard, and Splügen, and arrived in the rear of Melas. Moreau did not entirely conform to Napoleon's plan; he crossed the Rhine near Basle, where he was already in possession of a *tête-de-pont*, and, therefore, the campaign in Germany was not so decisive as that in Italy. Melas found himself turned, and was obliged to fight at Marengo, front against Austria; he was defeated, and consequently compelled to enter into a convention with Napoleon, by which the latter obtained the western portion of Italy as far as the Mincio. The battle of Marengo, and indeed the whole of Napoleon's manœuvres, took place only after he had received a reinforcement of fifteen thousand men from Moreau.

**Defensive Operations.**—We may act on the offensive even though the war be a defensive one for us. This will always be the case when we are ready to take the field before the enemy can; or when his dispositions are faulty, his army corps dispersed, etc., or when our numerical superiority is very great. The initiative is always advantageous, and the defensive only should be taken in case of inferiority in strength.

The defense, as well as the offensive, can act on simple or on several lines of operation; the plan of it is always more or less intimately connected with the configuration of the ground than that of the attack. In the defense, the natural or artificial obstacles of the country should supply the deficiency of men, either in strategical or in tactical operations. When acting on simple lines, and opposed only to one army, but that one superior, our own army should retreat, availing itself of all the natural obstacles of the theater of the war, such as rivers, mountains, etc.; it should organize small bodies for acting in the rear of the advancing enemy to endanger his convoys, and force him to send large detachments to cover them.

In making those detachments, the invading army becomes smaller the farther it advances, while, on the other hand, the defending army generally becomes stronger the nearer it approaches the center of its country. If by this the difference in force is decreased, and the chances rendered more equal, the army for the defense should pass to a vigorous offensive, either by unexpectedly attacking the enemy, or by awaiting him in a well chosen and strongly fortified position.

The campaign of 1812 is a fine example of such a defense. Napoleon entered Russia with 450,000 men. The Russian army retreated, defending only the town of Smolensk. Owing to the many corps Napoleon was obliged to leave behind to cover his communications, and to the losses already sustained, he arrived at Borodino with only 132,000 men. The Russians awaited him there with 117,000 men, in a partly fortified position. What was impossible against an army of 450,000 men could be tried against one of 132,000.

When the enemy has chosen two lines of operation, we may be inclined to take but one line of operation, and bring our army into a central position between his armies, so as to fall with our whole force on the first of his corps that presents itself, and then defeat the other. At the siege of Mantua, in 1796, Napoleon, being informed that Wurmser, who had advanced from the Tyrol against him, had divided his forces and was descending one bank of the Lake of Garda with his main body, while Quasdanowitch was descending the other, raised the siege of Mantua, advanced and stationed himself at one end of the lake, thereby gaining a central position, and, separating Wurmser from Quasdanowitch, the latter was defeated at Lonato and the former at Castiglione.

When obliged to form several lines of operation, we should arrange them in the following manner:—

If, for instance, 100,000 men are to resist an invading army of 150,000, divided into three armies of 50,000 each, we should divide our force also. We form three corps of observation, each numbering 15,000 men. We keep the remaining 55,000 in reserve, and transport them successively, by interior lines and forced marches, to the three army corps, and form every time a large army of 70,000 men, who should defeat the 50,000 opposed to them. The two remaining corps of observation, if pressed by their opponents, retreat, defending every inch of ground, but refusing open battle, till they are in turn reinforced by the reserve. In those cases the defense loses ground, but soon regains it.

If the enemy has formed double lines of operation very distant from each other, we should also form two lines, and retreat on concentric ones; when we arrive at such points that our armies are only a few days' march distant from each other, we should leave a corps of observation before one of the enemy's armies, in order to mask our movements, and, with our main body, reach by forced marches our other army, unite with it, and defeat the enemy by our superiority; we then return to the first army, the fate of which will not remain long undecided.

In 1796 the Archduke Charles, in Germany, defeated the armies of Jourdan and Moreau by retreating in concentric lines from the Rhine to the Bohemian frontier, where he united part of his two armies; he first defeated Jourdan at Amberg and Wurzburg, and then Moreau at Emmendingen and Schlingen.

During the war of 1758–1762, Frederick the Great was attacked by a Russian, Austrian, and German imperial army. He resisted those three armies by disposing his own on interior lines. He always transported the mass of his troops to the endangered point by means of those interior lines, and defeated the different hostile armies one after the other.

In the years 1813 and 1814 Napoleon, in his defense, likewise acted on interior lines.

These different rules have reference only to the movements and operations of one or more armies when once in the field, but they do not give the great *ensemble* of a war, nor do they reflect any light on the manner in which wars of a different character are to be conducted. The entire plan of a campaign would be different if the war were a civil one, a religious one, a distant conquest, or an invasion. There is but little resemblance between the campaigns of 1806 and those of the Peninsular war, though both were wars of conquest. The configuration of the theater of war, the character of the people, their government, and political circumstances being different, other means and plans became necessary. Wars of conquest and occupation being those which at the present moment interest us most, we will devote a few pages to them, and see how they have been carried on at different times by great captains.

**Wars of Conquest, or Great Invasions.**—The manner of making war, or even of conducting great invasions, has passed through various stages in the course of time.

Most of the wars recorded in ancient history were wars of conquest, in which entire populations were launched against others. Very early, however, we find the commencement of military organization, and even standing armies. By-and-by more and more complete systems were introduced. In the classic times of Greece, those of Philip of Macedon, and of his great son, Alexander, in the times when the Roman eagle began to spread its powerful wings over the then known world, the art of war attained to a perfection which has been surpassed only in modern times; and even the great masters of the art in later ages sought for wisdom and instruction in the deeds of the illustrious captains of antiquity.

The degeneracy of the Roman empire, the immense emigration of uncivilized hordes, the overthrow of Roman civilization, soon brought the art of war back to its childhood. In the time of the Crusades it is distinguished principally by the employment of large masses of combatants and brute force, which sometimes attains success, though void of art or skill.

All the great States of Europe, held by kings or emperors, were divided into a number of principalities, large or small, governed by petty chieftains, on whose good-will the chief rulers were more or less dependent. The consequence was, that all the governments of Europe were so much occupied in preserving internal order, that great invasions became almost impossible.

The times of Charles V., Francis II., and Henry IV. revived the art of war, and we see great captains appearing on the stage; but the political systems and circumstances of Europe did not change. In the times of Louis XIV. and Louis XV. we find wars, even by great captains, conducted in a slow and methodical manner, whence it was called "methodic warfare." Armies at that time lived in tents, camped, had vast magazines around and near them, and could not exist without an immense bakery close to their heels.

This was the state of affairs at the commencement of the French Revolution; but here the revolution made itself felt also. Immense armies being created, for which scarcely the necessary armament could be found, still less tents, camp equipage, and provision trains, it became necessary to quarter these armies in the towns and villages, in order to shelter and nourish them, and subsist them on the inhabitants. Movement was not only rendered easier by this system, but became a necessity, as no district could nourish for any length of time so great an accumulation of men. Consequently methodic warfare changed at once to rapid, daring marches, and manœuvres on a grand scale. The old indispensable bakery gave way to the famous Roman maxim, "War must nourish war."

The adoption of this great principle changed, as by magic, the entire system of warfare. Armies which had hitherto marched only five or six miles a day, now marched twenty or twenty-five. Where small operations, such as the taking of a fortress, or the conquest of a province, had satisfied the ambition of a general, we now see armies made to traverse hundreds of miles, and push right into the heart of an enemy's country.

Campaigns became more extended and more decisive. In a word, the reins were loosed, and intelligence, courage, enterprise, youth, and vigor were launched, without restraint, against the enemy. The system of quartering or living on the inhabitants of the land forms the basis of all great wars of conquest or invasion; unless it be adopted, it is impossible to conquer an extensive country possessing large and organized armies.

Let us draw a comparison between the efficiency of two armies—the one acting according to the principles of methodic warfare, and being furnished continually from its base of supply and its magazines, the other acting according to the principle, "War must nourish war."

In the first case, provisions for several days must always be carried with the army; immense supply trains have to follow it; bad roads—which would, however, have sufficed for the passage of troops—become impassable, in consequence of the transit of the immense number of heavily-laden wagons. Everywhere there is stoppage in the advance and starting of troops, obstruction of roads, delay, and disorder. As soon as the provisions in the wagons are consumed, or nearly so, the army halts. With immense trouble and cost, a fresh supply of provisions is obtained after a number of days; the army starts anew, but only to come to another halt as soon as its wagons are emptied again. But, then, another difficulty arises; the army is already so far from its base that the supply by wagons becomes impossible; the number of days the wagons require to be *en route* is too great; and in the mean time the army runs the risk of perishing from hunger. The consequence is, that an operation, whatever may be its strategic advantages, cannot be carried out, if it does not offer extraordinary means of communication with the base of supply; and it follows that, instead of choosing the most advantageous strategic lines as lines of operation, the most comfortable and convenient lines of communication are selected as the principal strategic direction to be given to the armies. In other words, the quartermaster and the commissary are in reality the commanders. The army cannot march where they forbid, nor can it move until they are ready or want to be so.

It is scarcely necessary to remark that, in consequence of the slow marching and the frequent halts in order to maintain the supply of provisions, the enemy gains ample time to prevent the success of any plan of operation, not to mention the inducement which such large wagon trains offer for cavalry raids in the rear of the army. Do away with this system of feeding the troops, and movement will become a necessity; the most advantageous strategic lines of operation can be chosen; there is no stoppage, except by the enemy; but this resistance is, under such circumstances, such as a general would desire. In other words, all that is impossible when following the old system, becomes possible with the new. Where two men can plant their feet, an army can march; and instead of months of operations, the campaign will take only as many weeks, or perhaps days.

I do not wish to advocate here a system of great and legally-organized robbery, which takes from the countryman all he has without any indemnification. I advocate only a reasonable and well-organized system of requisition, paying liberally for all it obtains, but furnishing the army with all the principal provisions from the country through which it passes. The greater the distance an army marches in one day, the more plentifully it may be supplied.

All wars of invasion or conquest, from the earliest times down to the most modern—from the Romans to Napoleon—were based upon, and rendered possible by, this principle alone. Successful wars of conquest are therefore synonymous with rapid and energetic operations. Let us pass in review some of the principal.

Conquering a country, means successfully fighting its defenders; subduing a country, means occupying it. Fighting means concentration, occupying means division of forces. Here is evidently the difficulty of wars of conquest. As long as only the army of the invaded country takes part in the struggle, an occupation is scarcely necessary till this army is really destroyed; but the moment the war against the invader becomes national, and the population takes part in it, matters become different and more difficult. In this latter case, the operating or field army should not be reduced by detachments, but the troops necessary for the occupation should be sent from the base of operations.

Three systems have been principally employed for the conquest of a country. The first, is to march several armies from the circumference into the center of a country; the second, is to conquer it by subduing and occupying one province after another; the third, is by marching one large force, on a single line of operation, right into the center of a country, and when arrived there, spreading it out in all directions, like a fan, forming interior lines, dividing thereby the enemy, and forcing him to act on exterior lines. It is the very inverse of the first system.

*The first system*, viz., that of acting with several armies from the circumference against the center of a country, has been spoken of above in treating of offensive and defensive operations. We have seen that, though each of the invading armies may be stronger than the one opposed to it, the defense has the advantage; because it acts on interior lines, and can unite its forces before the invading armies can unite theirs on the exterior lines, on which they are obliged to act.

The campaigns already mentioned of Frederick the Great—those of 1793, of 1796 in Germany, and of 1814—show to what disasters such concentric operations may conduct. However, it would be wrong to reject this system entirely; there are several cases in which it may be used with advantage. There is no danger in having several lines of operations in the three following cases: 1st. When each of the invading armies is equal in number to the whole defending force. 2d. When the invading armies are very large, so that the whole of them could not operate on one line, as was the case in 1813, in the campaign in Saxony against Napoleon. 3d. When the power attacked has no regular military system, and is not far advanced in the art of war.

*The second system*, that of conquering one province after another, is slow but sure. It was the great maxim followed by the Roman republic, and is identical in principle with that of dividing the enemy's forces and acting with the whole of our force against every one of its divisions separately. The conquered province is organized, receives an administration from the conqueror, and serves as a base of operation against the next or adjacent province.

This system, however, is generally only possible against States or people not well united, and suffering from internal dissensions. Napoleon made frequent use of it too; his kingdoms of Westphalia and of Italy, and the organization of the Rhine Bund, were applications of the Roman system of conquest, only executed in a much shorter time than was usual with the Romans. The only defense against such a system is the perfect union of all parts of a nation, and the full determination to resist the invader and every infraction of the country's rights.

*The third and last system* is evidently the most scientific, and best suited for rapid and decisive invasions. It was used by Cesar in his Gallic war, and by Napoleon in most of his continental invasions. It consisted in concentrating for the battle and dividing after it, so as to destroy all smaller resisting armies and complete the victory. The following is the plan of operations:—

The army, in one compact mass, enters the enemy's country, where it at first finds resistance. This, by the great superiority of numbers, is overpowered; the road into the heart of the invaded country is thrown open; the victorious army follows it with impetuosity; and, arrived in the center of the theater of war, fills up the whole area by spreading out in all directions. All local resistance is broken; the smaller army corps of the invaded country, being pushed back in all directions, and separated from each other by the heavy mass of the enemy's forces acting on interior lines, cannot offer any resistance of moment; and thus a country, rich in all kinds of resources, may be obliged to make an ignominious peace with an enemy more skillful, but not stronger than itself.

The campaigns of 1805, 1806, and 1809, and also the campaigns of 1808 in the Peninsular war, are models for similar invasions. The ultimate success of those plans is founded on a first great victory obtained by rapid and unexpected manœuvres. The defense against an attack so directed may be of two kinds, either of which may be adopted according to circumstances. In both cases, the grand necessity is to avoid a first disaster.

The campaign of 1812 is an example of one of those cases of defense. The defensive army retreats, being continually reinforced; the invading army, by advancing, is proportionally weakened. When an equality or superiority of force has been obtained, the defense passes to the offensive; and the greater the effort of the invading army at first—that is, the longer the line of operation, and consequently its line of retreat—the surer will be its total destruction.

The retreat from Moscow is a proof of this. In 1809 Napoleon, in the first onset, obtained but a partial success—that is, instead of destroying, he only defeated the armies of the Archduke Charles in the battles of Landshut, Eckmühl, and Ratisbon. The bloody check he received a short time afterward at Esslingen was the consequence of this imperfect success. Had Napoleon, in the Russian campaign, been able to destroy the Russian army at first—and he tried hard to do so—the disasters of Krasnoi and the Beresina would not have happened.

All countries do not offer the facility of retreating indefinitely, like that possessed by Russia. Those that do not, must have recourse to other means. The surest is an extended system of fortifications similar to the famous Austrian quadrilateral in Italy. Fortifications forming double *têtes-de-pont* are points of strategic importance; and forming at the same time large intrenched camps, they cannot be passed or taken in a hurry by an invading army. The defending army, basing itself on one or other of these fortifications, can attack the front, flank, and rear of the invaders. Large corps of observation must be left before these works, or a regular siege must be undertaken. Time is gained, and this is what the defense principally requires, in order to collect its means and to commence offensive operations against the invading army, for which this system of fortification, as well as the necessitated division of the enemy, offers the best chance of success. As already said, in operating on this plan, a first disaster must be avoided, as well as in the case mentioned before.

All these invasive wars are, or ought to be, undertaken by greatly superior armies. Brilliant manœuvres, like those of Jena and Ulm, were only executed with vastly superior numbers. In general, there exists a relation between the extent of a country, its geographical features, and the number of troops necessary to invade it, or, at least, to render strategic operations successful. The larger and flatter a country is, the less marked features it possesses; the greater the number of roads passing through it in all directions, the less applicability will the maxims of strategy have.

In his campaigns in Russia, we see Napoleon continually baffled in his strenuous and repeated efforts to capture or destroy even a part of the Russian army, though his army was immense—not less than 450,000 men. The country was still greater; Russian and French columns passed and repassed each other without being informed of it till too late. In Spain we find similar effects arising from similar causes. In Italy, on the contrary, nearly every operation was a success; the reason being that the roads were comparatively few, the theater of operations limited, and the strategic features of the country remarkable.

We might enumerate many campaigns whose failure is attributable to the fact that the number of troops was insufficient for the extent of the theater of war. The Russian and Peninsular campaigns are of the number; so are the campaigns of the English in America.

The number of troops depends not only upon the extent and the geography of the country, but also upon the more or less warlike character of the population, political influence, etc. As a general rule, I believe it may be laid down that, for a great invasion, the front of operation should extend entirely over at least one zone of the theater of war; and in this front, the different columns of march should be at proper supporting distance from each other.—(See *Logistics*, pages 173–182, "Summary of the Art of War.")

After having passed in review the geographical features of the Southern Confederacy, we will apply the different principles, maxims, and rules just laid down to the present war; and thereby give a more exact idea of the mode in which wars of conquest ought to be conducted.

# II.

## GEOGRAPHY OF THE SOUTHERN CONFEDERACY.

The Southern Confederacy, at the outbreak of the war, consisted of the States of Virginia, North and South Carolina, Georgia, Florida, Alabama, Mississippi, Tennessee, Kentucky, Missouri, Arkansas, Louisiana, and Texas.

The principal boundaries were, on the east, the ocean; on the south, the Gulf of Mexico; on the west, Mexico and the Territories; and on the north, the Ohio and the Potomac. The Mississippi, in its upper course, formed the line of separation between Missouri and Illinois.

Those boundaries inclose an immense tract of land, and, at first, one is at a loss to determine at which point to attack the colossus. Strategy, for its appliance, however, demands an analysis of the country similar to that which the surgeon undertakes of a limb for his anatomical studies, or a chemist of a mineral substance. All that seems complicated is, by such an analysis, divided and separated into its elements; and the confusion which the *ensemble* at first creates in our mind passes away and gives place to more enlightened and properly digested views.

The great features of a country are furnished by its boundaries, and by the form and direction of its mountain chains and its rivers. Those three elements combined generally determine the direction of the principal lines of communication as well as the situation of the chief centers of population.

We have already seen that every country or theater of war can be divided into three distinct zones—right, left, and center. In most cases the natural lines of separation of these three zones are strongly marked. One of them always offers greater strategical advantages than the other two, and we should, therefore, select it to carry on operations in.

Considering then this zone as a theater of war by itself, it may in its turn be subdivided into right, left, and center zones. Let us in this way divide the Southern Confederacy and see what we obtain.

Looking at it from north to south, we detect at once some prominent features. To the right we see the Mississippi dividing it and separating a large part from the main body of it. To the left we remark a long mountain chain separating the country this side of the Mississippi into two parts.

The country beyond the Mississippi, composed principally of Missouri, Arkansas, and Louisiana, forms the *Right Zone* of the whole theater of war. The large river separating it from the rest of the Confederacy renders communication with this latter difficult, and may even interrupt military operations entirely.

The country east of the above-mentioned mountain chains, called the Blue Ridge and the Alleghanies, forms the *Left Zone.* It is principally composed of Virginia, North Carolina, and South Carolina. The mountains form the northwest boundary, the Potomac the northeast, the Savannah the southwest, and the ocean the southeast boundary of this zone.

Finally, the country between the right and the left zone forms the *Center Zone* of the theater of war. It is composed of Kentucky, Tennessee, Mississippi, Alabama, Georgia, and Florida; its boundaries are the Ohio, the Mississippi, the Gulf of Mexico, the ocean, and the Savannah River.

We have to consider these three zones in detail.

**Left Zone.**—This zone forms a kind of quadrangle, two sides of which are formed by the Savannah River and the Potomac line from Harper's Ferry to Cape Hatteras. The other two sides are formed, the one by the coast from Cape Hatteras to the mouth of the Savannah, the other by the mountains from Harper's Ferry to Pickens.

This zone is about 400 miles long, and about 250 wide.

The direction of the two long sides of the quadrangle, that is of the coast and the mountains, is from northeast to southwest.

**Mountains.**—The mountains which form the boundary of this zone are part of the long mountain chain passing nearly through the whole of the northern continent. Commencing at Montreal and Quebec, they run in a nearly continuous chain from northeast to southwest as far as the north of Georgia; there they change their course, taking a direction from east to west, and falling gradually as they approach the Mississippi.

The characteristic of this mountain chain is that it is formed by a number of long and parallel ridges; there are, comparatively, very few offshoots having a course at right angles to the main direction.

These parallel ridges are very numerous in the north of Virginia. Some of them form between them wide and fertile valleys. In the south of Virginia and the east of Tennessee they become fewer and approach each other nearer, forming thereby long and narrow valleys.

Most of these valleys are watered by rivers, nearly all of which are rapid; many of them rapid and deep, as, for instance, the Shenandoah, the Upper James River, the Holston, etc. etc.

The communications from one valley to another, over the mountains, are few, and generally difficult. There are, however, a number of roads by which one can pass from Western Virginia into Eastern Virginia or North Carolina.

The most important and most continuous of these ridges is the chain which, under the name of Loudon Heights, Blue Ridge, etc., runs nearly without interruption from one end of the left zone to the other. West of this chain is a large number of parallel chains; east of it is one range more, commencing with the Kittoctan Mountains on the Potomac, and having its termination in the Bull Run Mountains, Pig Nut Mountains, Southwest Mountains, Carter's Mountains, Buffalo Ridge, etc. etc.

The number of gaps in Blue Ridge Mountain is small; the principal ones are Vestal, Snicker's, Ashby's, Manassas, Chester, Thornton's, Swift Run, Simon's, Brown's, Rockfish, White's, Robenton's, Petit's, Bufford's, Daniel's Run, etc. etc. The eastern ridge, being formed by the isolated hills or ridges above named, has as many gaps as there are ridges. With the exception of Thoroughfare Gap, in Bull Run Mountains, there is no other worth mentioning.

Of the valleys formed by these mountains three are of great importance. First, the Shenandoah valley; then, the valley formed by Blue Ridge and the Eastern Mountains, commencing with Loudon valley and going down as far as Lynchburg; and, thirdly, the valley in which the railroad from Lynchburg to Chattanooga is laid down.

The greater portion of the country in this zone is hilly, with the exception of the districts near the sea-shore, where large plains and swamps are to be found.

**Rivers.**—Besides the Shenandoah, there are some smaller streams situated in the valleys parallel to the Shenandoah valley. Those in North Virginia are tributaries of the Potomac; they are, with the exception of the Shenandoah, of little importance. The upper part of the James River runs for a certain length in the valleys behind Blue Ridge, and so does the higher part of the Roanoke. The rivers in the valleys of South Virginia take a southwesterly course; they are tributaries of the Tennessee River.

All the other rivers having their rise in the mountains have a course more or less parallel to the Potomac; that is to say, running from the mountains nearly direct to the sea in a direction parallel to the two smaller sides of the quadrangle forming the left zone. Most of these rivers form at their mouths long and deep bays, some of them penetrating for eighty or more miles into the interior of the country. The Potomac, the Rappahannock, the York, and the James Rivers, Albemarle and Pamlico Sounds and Port Royal entrance, deserve to be mentioned. These bays offer to ships-of-war and transports great facilities for penetrating into the interior, and may be advantageously made use of in military operations.

The principal rivers, beginning with the north, are—

1. The *Potomac*—navigable for the heaviest kinds of ships as far as Alexandria, and for somewhat lighter ships up to Washington. Above Washington it is fordable in several places. From Washington to Harper's Ferry the Potomac averages several hundred yards in width. The banks are generally hilly.

2. *Bull Run*—already notorious in the history of this war. This river is, in the dry season, passable in most places, but it may, nevertheless, serve as a defensive line against an enemy coming from the north, and has already been used as such. It rises in the Bull Run Mountains, and its whole course is about forty miles, but the lower part assumes somewhat of the character of a bay, and is, therefore, difficult to cross.

3. The *Rappahannock* takes its rise in the Blue Ridge Mountains; it has a total length of about one hundred and thirty miles, of which, however, about seventy are to be considered as a bay. The river is navigable up to Fredericksburg. Ten miles above it divides, and is called the Hedgeman River and the Rapidan; both are fordable at a great many points, and trestle bridges may be constructed at nearly any point without much difficulty. The banks are hilly, and at some parts are so even to the water's edge, but in other parts leaving plains between the river and the ascent. Some excellent defensive positions are to be found, as, for instance, those near Fredericksburg.

4. The *York River*—navigable up to West Point; there it divides into the Mattapony River and the Pamunkey River, which latter, in its turn, is formed by the junction of the North Anna River and the South Anna River. The entire length of the whole water-course is about one hundred and twenty miles. The springs are situated in the Southwest Mountains. All three rivers are available for defense.

5. The *Chickahominy.*—An army coming from Fredericksburg, and marching to Richmond, would have to cross this little creek, which has already obtained great celebrity in the campaign of the past summer. Its swampy banks and moving ground render the construction of bridges a matter of great difficulty.

6. The *James River* is a large river, navigable up to Richmond. Its course is about four hundred miles. It cuts through the Blue Ridge, and rises in one of the western ridges. The banks are very hilly, and may be easily defended. The James River and the York River, this last and the Rappahannock, and this again with the Potomac, form three large peninsulas, about fifty miles long and ten to twenty miles wide. From Richmond to City Point, about eighteen miles in a straight line, the James River has a nearly southern course. At City Point

7. The *Appomattox River* empties into the James River. The Appomattox is navigable up to Petersburg; its course is parallel to that of the James River, has a length of about one hundred miles, and rises near Clover Hill.

8. The *Chowan River* divides into the Nottaway River and the Meherin River; its whole course amounts to about one hundred and twenty miles. The Chowan River empties into Albemarle Sound.

9. The *Roanoke*, a considerable river, is formed by the junction of the Dan and the Staunton Rivers, both rapid mountain streams; the former rises in Blue Ridge, the latter in North Mountain. The entire course of the Roanoke is about 300 miles; it empties into Albemarle Sound, and is navigable for Sound craft as far as thirty miles, and for boats still farther up.

10. The *Tar River* empties into Pamlico Sound.

11. The *Neuse River* empties into Pamlico Sound, has a length of about 180 miles. Navigable up to Newbern.

12. The *Cape Fear River* empties, near Wilmington, into the ocean; the depth of water at the bar is from twelve to fifteen feet. The length of its course is about 280 miles. Its course is much more southerly than that of the James River.

13. The *Great Pedee River* empties, near Georgetown, in Wingaw Bay. Its course is nearly north to south, and its length about 380 miles. It is navigable by steam-boats up to Cheraw; above this place there is a fall of fifteen feet in eighteen miles.

14. The *Santee River* is formed by the junction of the Catawba and Congaree. The length of its course is about 400 miles. Steam-boats ascend as far as Camden and Columbia; and by means of canal-boats navigation is carried on up to the mountains. It has very swampy banks, and empties, near the Great Pedee, into the ocean.

15. The *Edisto River* empties near Charleston. Its length is about 200 miles.

16. The *Savannah* empties into Tybee Sound. The

length of its course is over 400 miles. The direction of its course is from northwest to southeast. It rises in the mountains of North Carolina, and is formed by the junction of two branches. It is navigable for steamers up to Augusta, and for large ships up to Savannah.

Most of the rivers mentioned above are subject to rapid rising; and, in consequence of the bays which many of them form, the tide is felt at a great distance inland.

It is easy to see that these rivers could be used with advantage as lines of defense against an enemy coming from the north.

The principal towns are—

**In Virginia.**—Harper's Ferry, Winchester, Staunton, Woodstock, Leesburg, Warrenton, Gordonsville, Lynchburg, Fredericksburg, Richmond, Petersburg, Norfolk, and Portsmouth.

**In North Carolina.**—Wilmington, Fayetteville, Raleigh, Newbern, Greenville, and Smithville, etc.

**In South Carolina.**—Columbia, Charleston, Georgetown, Beaufort, and Pickens.

Some of these places are of a certain strategic importance. For instance, Winchester, Gordonsville, Lynchburg, Fredericksburg, Richmond, Petersburg, Wilmington, Charleston, and Pickens.

**Lines of Communication.**—We have to distinguish those running parallel with the different rivers—that is to say, joining the mountains with the sea-shore—and those running parallel with the mountain chains. To the first class belong, to a certain extent, all the navigable rivers, besides the railroads from—1. Manassas to Woodstock, 60 miles.

2. Staunton to Gordonsville, 55 miles; and to Sexton Junction, 40 miles; total, 95 miles. 3. West Point to Richmond, 30 miles; to Lynchburg, 112 miles; and to Chattanooga, 420 miles, total, 562 miles. 4. Norfolk to Petersburg, 80 miles; and to Lynchburg, 110 miles; total, 190. 5. Norfolk to Suffolk, 20 miles; to Weldon, 60 miles; to Clarksville, 55 miles; and to Danville, 48 miles; total, 173 miles. 6. Beaufort, N. C., to Goldsborough, 90 miles; to Raleigh, 48 miles; and to Greensborough, 75 miles; total, 213 miles. 7. Wilmington to Columbia, 180 miles; and to Pickens, 140 miles; 320 miles. 8. Charleston to Augusta, 120 miles; to Chattanooga, 300 miles; total, 420 miles.

Besides these railroads, there is a great number of turnpikes and roads running in the same direction. The greatest number of these roads have for their object the uniting of the sea-ports with the interior of the country.

The number of railroads passing through the country in a longitudinal direction is more restricted. We can only name those from—1. Fredericksburg to Richmond, 60 miles; and Wilmington, 240 miles; total, 300 miles. 2. Richmond to Salisbury, 220 miles; to Columbia, 140 miles; and to Charleston, 125 miles; total, 485 miles. 3. Wilmington to Florence, 100 miles; and to Charleston, 110 miles; total, 210 miles. 4. Charleston to Savannah, 100 miles. 5. Lynchburg to Chattanooga, 420 miles.

Also in this direction there is no want of turnpikes and other roads. These roads, though bad and very different from a French imperial turnpike, are, nevertheless, passable by troops of all arms; and as there are a great number of parallel roads—perhaps more than in any European country of equal magnitude—large armies may be moved in parallel columns with ease and celerity, supposing, however, that the season is not too wet.

In the direction of the longitudinal roads there is one thing worthy of remark, and of high strategic importance. It is this: that most of these roads end at the sea-coast. The direction of the Richmond and Wilmington, or Richmond and Charleston Railroad line, for instance, is not parallel with the mountain chain or the sea-coast, but cut diagonally across the country. The result is, that an army placed at or near Lynchburg would prevent, by marching straight south, any Rebel army placed at Richmond and trying to escape, from doing so. An army moving south from Lynchburg would arrive at Georgetown or Charleston; an army moving south from Richmond would arrive at Wilmington. If both armies have moved with equal speed, the latter would therefore find the enemy established on its line of retreat, and itself thrown back on the sea in case of defeat.

As a general observation, it may be said here that the country of this zone is sufficiently populous to sustain an army on its through march, if moved on parallel roads.

After having thus passed this zone in review, let us examine what facilities or difficulties it offers to the operations of a large army. To facilitate this investigation, let us consider it as a theater in itself, and divide it accordingly into three zones—right, left, and center.

These three zones are strongly enough marked to be distinguished at once. Blue Ridge Mountain, with its few gaps, effectually separates the principal mountain district from the rest of the zone. All west of the Blue Ridge will therefore be the right zone of our restricted theater of war. The more eastern ridge, formed by the Kittoctan, Bull Run, and Southwest Mountains, separates the valley, running from Berlin, on the Potomac, down to Lynchburg, on the James River, from the eastern part of Virginia. This valley therefore forms the center zone. Finally, all east of the center zone will be contained in the left.

Now, an army can operate in one of these three zones alone, or in two combined. An army operating in the right zone can do so by taking the Potomac as a base of operation, and advancing along the valleys; or, by taking the Ohio as a base, and passing through Western Virginia or Eastern Tennessee over the mountains. An army taking the Upper Potomac as a base of operation, and advancing along the valleys, would probably find little difficulty in doing so. We have seen the whole Rebel army marching from Martinsburg down these valleys, and maintaining itself there for a long while.

To use the position of this zone to advantage, the first necessity is evidently to have continual control of the mountain gaps leading into the center zone. The mountains themselves are most of them steep, rugged, and wooded, and can only be crossed by these gaps, which are easily defensible. In all parts of these valleys an army on a rapid march might find enough to subsist on.

An army marching from the Ohio, as a base of operation, into Virginia or North or South Carolina, would find more difficulties, as it would have to cross a number of parallel ridges, as well as to pass through districts thinly inhabited, and where provisions consequently are scarce. But even this might be accomplished with an army not too large, and composed of good material, considering that the main distance over the mountains is not over seventy or eighty miles; and ought, therefore, to be accomplished in from four to five days.

An army operating in the center zone has still greater facilities for moving than in the right. In this zone all the rivers have their source, and are therefore inconsiderable, and do not form obstacles of any importance to an advancing army. The possession of the gaps to the right, as well as to the left, is of the utmost importance; and remembering this, it would appear that a combined movement in the two zones—right and center—would be most advantageous, considering that all the gaps would then easily fall.

The strategic importance of Lynchburg, at the end of the valley forming this zone, we have already noticed, when speaking of the lines of communication. An army marching through this zone may be maintained in it, if no long halts be made in any particular place. A number of parallel roads facilitates the movement of a large army in marching in parallel columns. The roads are of the character already spoken of.

Both right and center zones offer difficulties the moment the army is to be provisioned from its base of operations, the Potomac; though even there arrangements may be made and intermediary depots created which would facilitate its subsistence.

An army operating in the left zone can operate in two ways: either by marching down from the Potomac—that is to say, taking the Potomac as the base of operation; or by making use of the maritime facilities, and by disembarking a large force at any point of the coast.

The first plan—that of marching from the Potomac down to the Savannah in the left zone, which is near the sea-coast—has this disadvantage: it offers the enemy all strategical and tactical advantages; the fifteen rivers to be crossed are so many lines of defense. On the other hand, the deep and large bays facilitating navigation in this zone, would facilitate the provisioning of an army.

The second plan—that of disembarking a large force on any point of the coast—would experience, in a southerly or northerly movement, the same tactical and strategical difficulties as an army moving from the Potomac, as a base of operation, would, though the number of those difficulties may be reduced; but others, growing out of the very nature of such a combined—that is to say, half naval and half military—operation, would arise; and as a whole, the difficulties would probably not be less in the one case than in the other.

There are other considerations rendering the use of this zone less convenient than that of the two others; they will be explained in discussing the operations of the campaign.

We may remark here that an expedition may be accomplished with comparative ease, considering the nature of the coast, and that the provisioning of troops would be greatly facilitated by it. Most, or nearly all, of the important cities of the main left zone *are on its left;* even the capital of the whole Confederacy is situated there. These seem great inducements for its choice as the principal zone of operation. How far this is correct, we shall see.

**Center Zone.**—This zone is formed, as we have already seen, by the States of Kentucky, Tennessee, Mississippi, Alabama, Georgia, and Florida. The Big Sandy River, Cumberland Mountains, Savannah River, and ocean are the boundaries on the east; the Gulf of Mexico on the south; the Mississippi on the west; and the Ohio on the north.

This zone has a peculiarity which must be noticed and well understood; for the success of all military operations depends upon it. It is, that this zone is divided into two entirely distinct parts by the Tennessee River, each part forming a theater of war in itself. The upper part, comprising Kentucky, Tennessee, and a small portion of North Alabama, is inclosed between the waters of the Tennessee River, the Ohio, and the Big Sandy Rivers. The Tennessee River nearly describes a semicircle. Where it rises, it runs parallel with the mountains—that is, from northeast to southwest. At Chattanooga it changes direction, following a clear westerly course; and at Florence it turns northward, and keeps in this direction to its mouth. The country inclosed by it and by the Ohio, we will call the upper center zone; and the country south of the Tennessee, or rather the remainder of the center zone, we will call the lower center zone. The lower center zone is principally distinguished from the upper one by the course of its rivers, which all run southward and empty into the Gulf, instead of emptying northward, as those of the upper center zone do. Let us consider these two parts of the center zone separately.

**Upper Center Zone.**—If we give to this zone part of Western Virginia, we form a kind of quadrangle, which, in a strategic point of view, presents great resemblance to the main left zone. In fact, one of the long sides of the quadrangle is formed by a mountain chain, the same which we have already encountered in the left zone; the other long or parallel side is formed by the Ohio, which plays the same part that the sea plays in the left zone. It is a natural obstacle to all movements of troops, except for the party having entire control of it. The two smaller sides are formed by the Lower Tennessee and the Big Sandy Rivers. The western part of this zone is very mountainous.

**Mountains.**—The Blue Ridge and its parallel ridges, on entering this zone, take a course a little more westward than in the north and west of Virginia. The Blue Ridge forms still the ridge at the east; the other parallel ridges, forming four main chains, are: Unaka, Great Smoky, Iron Mountain, Ray's Mountain, Clinch Mountain, and Cumberland Mountain. West from Cumberland Gap, the Cumberland Ridge becomes wider, and forms a kind of table-land. The main ridge also takes a more southerly direction, and thereby encounters the Tennessee River near Chattanooga, where the river breaks through it. South from the Tennessee, the mountains take a westerly direction, and lose themselves in smaller hills; forming, however, the separation between rivers running north and south.

From the Cumberland Mountains a number of offshoots start at right angles to the direction of the main chain; these advance far into Kentucky. Some of them form a kind of table-land. They give to the whole country a mountainous and rugged appearance; and they form parallel valleys, most of which are watered by the tributaries and confluents of the Licking and Kentucky Rivers.

**Gaps.**—The principal gaps are the Cumberland Gap, between Tazewell and Lafontaine, and some gaps in Great Smoky Mountain; one, for instance, near Ashbyville, the other, where the Little Tennessee River breaks through this mountain.

The main chains or ridges form long valleys, in which the Tennessee and Cumberland Rivers, or their principal confluents, run for a long distance.

There are no other mountains of importance in this zone. The western part is undulated, and in some places even flat, though bordered by ranges of hills which might, perhaps, serve as defensive positions, but which are, in fact, of no strategic importance whatever.

**Rivers.**—All the rivers of this upper center zone are tributaries of the Ohio. The main direction of the course of these rivers is from southeast to northwest, or rather northwest by north. However, the quasi-circular course of the Tennessee is more or less common to the other rivers, especially to those emptying into the Lower Ohio. Hence the Cumberland Gap is a kind of center, whence one might enter any of the valleys formed by the different rivers without being obliged to traverse the latter. In other words, most of the river valleys radiate more or less in the direction of the Cumberland Gap, the Ohio forming the circumference. The principal rivers are—

1. *Big Sandy River*, forming the boundary of Kentucky against Western Virginia. It rises in the Cumberland

Mountains, and has a course of about 120 miles. It runs in a valley formed by offshoots of the Cumberland Mountains, having a direction southeast by south and northwest by north. A road leads from the Ohio to Marion or Abingdon, on the East Tennessee and Virginia Railroad.

2. *Licking River* empties opposite Cincinnati. It rises in the Cumberland Mountains. Its course is somewhat more westerly than that of the Big Sandy River. It also runs in a valley formed by offshoots from the Cumberland Mountains. Its whole course is about 180 miles. It is navigable for boats for about 100 miles.

3. *Kentucky River.*—This is larger than the other two. The upper part of its course runs nearly west, and the lower nearly north. It rises in the Cumberland Mountains. The length of its course is about 250 miles. It is a rapid stream, in a deep, rocky bed, with steep banks. At high water it is navigable with steam-boats up to Frankfort, Ky., and with boats some 80 miles higher up.

4. *Rolling Fork* and *Salt River* unite together, rise in the middle of the State, carry a great amount of water, and are navigable for boats for about 100 miles.

5. *Green River* shapes its course according to that of the Tennessee River. It rises in the middle of the State; has very deep water. Steam-boats run up as far as Bowling Green, and for boats it is navigable nearly to its springs. Its entire length is about 225 miles.

6. *Cumberland River* rises in the Cumberland Mountains. Its course is shaped to that of the Tennessee River, the latter forming an exterior, and the Cumberland River an interior arc. It empties into the Ohio near Smithland,

about 15 miles from the mouth of the Tennessee. The length of its course is about 600 to 700 miles. It is navigable for steam-boats as far as Nashville, or about 160 miles, and in the wet season, with high water, as far as Burkesville. With boats it is navigable much higher up.

7. *Tennessee River* is formed by the junction of the Clinch and Holston Rivers, rising in the Alleghany Mountains of Virginia. Of its course we have already spoken. Its entire length is about 700 to 800 miles. It is navigable up to Florence, which is about 200 miles, and by boats it is navigable even up to the mountain district.

The principal towns are—

**In Kentucky.**—Covington, Louisville, Frankfort, Lexington, Lebanon, Bowling Green, Burkesville, Hopkinsville.

**In Tennessee.**—Dover, Clarksville, Nashville, Murfreesborough, Knoxville, Tazewell, Chattanooga.

**In North Alabama.**—Florence, Athens, Huntsville.

**Principal Lines of Communication.**—The principal lines of communication, running from northeast to southwest, are: 1. The Ohio. 2. The East Tennessee and Virginia Railroad, or from Memphis to Chattanooga, 300 miles, and from this place to Lynchburg, 420 miles; total, 720 miles.

Besides these two principal lines, there are smaller ones, such as the railroad from—1. Lexington to Louisville, 75 miles. 2. Memphis Junetion to Dover, 90 miles. 3. McMinnville to Tullahoma, 40 miles. 4. Tracy City to Fayetteville, 45 miles.

Of communication from north to south, we have to mention, besides the lower course of all the tributaries of the

Ohio, the following railroads: 1. Cincinnati to Lexington, 90 miles. 2. Louisville to Nashville, 175 miles. 3. Henderson to Nashville, 130 miles. 4. Nashville to Decatur, on the Tennessee, 110 miles. 5. Nashville to Stevenson, 100 miles.

A great number of turnpikes and other roads exist, traversing the country in all directions. Many of them run parallel to the different rivers, and therefore radiate in the direction of Cumberland Gap, or even of Chattanooga. This conformation renders these two points of great strategic interest.

Among the principal turnpikes and ordinary roads are those running along the valleys, and parallel to the Cumberland Mountains, besides the road from Tazewell to Lexington, and all those crossing the mountain chain. These roads are much the same as those of Virginia. The country in general is fertile, and in certain parts—for instance, the Kentucky valley—is very much so. It is therefore possible to maintain an army on its through march, if this army makes no long stoppage in any particular place.

If we consider now this upper center zone as a theater of war in itself, we should, in order to discuss the facilities of moving troops, have to divide it into three zones, as we did for the left main zone. Here, however, nature has not made the divisions so marked as in the first zone. Nevertheless, we can easily find such divisions as will suit our purpose, viz.: 1. The country east from Kentucky River, besides the whole mountain district, forms the left. 2. The country between Kentucky and Green River forms the center. 3. The country between Green River and Tennessee forms the right.

Of these three zones, the latter or right is evidently the most accessible or easy to pass through. Two rivers, navigable up to the end of this zone, besides the Henderson and Nashville Railroad, form as many good lines of communication for an army having the Lower Ohio as a base of operation. In marching south into Tennessee, it is only necessary to have control of the two rivers by means of gun-boats. Large numbers of troops may be very rapidly transported on these two rivers; and this is a great advantage, besides the facility of being supplied by three roads which also join the main road from the center zone, being the Louisville and Nashville Railroad.

The center zone offers the same advantages for supplying troops, except that in moving them forward they could not be transported by water. This zone meeting the right zone, could, for supplying the army, make use of the means of transportation belonging to the latter.

By marching in the center zone, however, a certain number of rivers would have to be crossed, which might serve a retreating enemy as lines of defense; and, in fact, have already been used as such. Combined operations in the left and center zones, however, would render this defense useless.

The most difficult to operate in, but probably the most important, is evidently the left zone. Full of mountains, rivers, without railroads, and only bad roads to march on, this zone offers, besides these disadvantages, a nearly impassable barrier, in the Cumberland Mountains, to an army advancing from north to south; and an army marching from Big Sandy River, parallel with the Cumberland Mountains, in the direction of Nashville, has a number of parallel ridges and rivers to cross. Could, however, such an army penetrate into the parallel valleys, such as the Cumberland, the Clinch, and the Holston, its advance would find no (or only small) difficulties, except, perhaps, in so far as provisioning is concerned.

The operations in this part of the upper center zone could only be carried on upon a limited number of roads; but precisely, in consequence of this small number, they (the operations) would be the more decisive. To pass from the left to the right zone—that is, from Chattanooga to Nashville, or the reverse—several roads may be found; but the Tennessee River, as well as several of the parallel chains, must be passed.

**The Lower Center Zone** is composed of part of Tennessee and Kentucky, and the whole of Mississippi, Alabama, Georgia, and Florida. The Savannah, Atlantic, the Mexican Gulf, the Mississippi, the Ohio, and the Tennessee inclose it between their waters.

There are no mountains of importance in this zone, except in the north of Georgia, in which the end of the Blue Ridge Mountains is to be found. From the highest point of this zone the fall is in all directions. We also see the principal rivers rise there, and take a southeasterly, southerly, southwesterly, and some, in their higher course, even a nearly westerly direction. Hilly offshoots of the highest part of this zone form the water-line between the Ohio and the Gulf.

The country in the north of Georgia consists partly of table-land, and the eastern ridge is still called the Blue Ridge. The remainder of the zone is partly undulating, partly flat. The country is watered by a great number of rivers, most of them running in a southerly direction, with the exception of some of the smaller tributaries of the Mississippi, which run from east to west. The principal rivers are—

1. The *Ogechee River.*—Its course is parallel to that of the Savannah. It empties itself into Ossabaw Sound. Its length is about 180 miles, of which about 40 miles are navigable for small vessels.

2. The *Alatamaha* empties into Alatamaha Sound. It is formed by the junction of the Oconee and Ocmulgee, both of which rise in the northern portion of the State. Their total length is about 300 miles; and they are navigable for steam-boats as far as Macon and Milledgeville.

3. The *Santilla* empties into St. Andrew's Sound. It passes through a swampy region, and is navigable only for light boats. Length about 150 miles.

4. The *Suwanee* empties into the Gulf of Mexico near Cedar Keys. Its length is about 250 miles.

5. *Apalachicola* empties into St. George's Sound. It is formed by the junction of the Flint and Chattahoochee Rivers. The latter rises in the Blue Ridge Mountains, and passes through the whole of this zone. It is navigable up to the Falls of Columbus, about 250 miles. The whole length is about 500 miles. Flint River rises in a hilly country south of the Chattahoochee, where also the Oconee and Ocmulgee rise. Its course is about 300 miles; navigable for about 75 miles.

6. The *Choctawhatchee River* empties into the bay of the same name, and is about 200 miles long.

7. The *Mobile River* is formed, about 50 miles above the Bay of Mobile, by the junction of the Alabama and Tombigbee. This latter receives a large confluent, the Black Warrior. Steam-boats go up on the Black Warrior as far as Tuscaloosa, 280 miles from its mouth; and on the Tombigbee as far as Columbus, on the Mississippi, a distance of 300 miles. The whole length of the Tombigbee is about 450 miles. The Alabama is navigable for steam-boats as far as Montgomery, about 300 miles.

8. The *Pascagoula* empties into the Mississippi Sound. It is navigable for about 100 miles. Its whole course extends over about 200 miles.

9. The *Pearl River* rises in the center of the State of Mississippi. It has a course of about 300 miles, and empties into the outlet of Lake Pontchartrain.

10. The *Mississippi* forms the western boundary of the zone.

Emptying into the Mississippi, and having partly a westward course, are—

11. The *Homochitto River.*

12. The *Yazoo River*, running, for a great distance, nearly parallel with the Mississippi.

13. *Big Black River.*

14. *Hatchie River.*

15. *Forked Deer River.*

16. *Obion River.*

The principal towns are—

**In Western Kentucky and Tennessee.**—Columbus, Paducah, Hickman, Paris, Huntingdon, Jackson, Bolivar, and Memphis.

**In Mississippi.**—Jackson, Natchez, Vicksburg, Columbus, Aberdeen, Holly Springs, Jacinto, Pearlington, Shieldsborough, Mississippi City, Biloxi, Pascagoula.

**In Alabama.**—Montgomery, Tuscaloosa, Mobile.

**In Georgia.**—Milledgeville, Augusta, Savannah, Columbus, Macon, Athens, Atlanta, Griffin.

**In Florida.**—Pensacola, Tallahassee, Apalachicola, San Augustine, Key West.

**Principal Lines of Communication.**—Most of the rivers serve as lines of communication in a direction from north to south. Besides these, there are railroads running in the same direction:—1. Paducah to Union City, 55 miles. 2. Cairo to Grand Junction, on the Memphis and Charleston road, 135 miles. 3. Cairo to Corinth, 150 miles. 4. Cairo to Memphis, 160 miles. 5. Memphis to New Orleans, 390 miles. 6. Grand Junction to Grenada, 90 miles. 7. Corinth to Mobile, 320 miles. 8. Montgomery to Pensacola, 165 miles. 9. Chattanooga to Atlanta, 120 miles. 10. Atlanta to Montgomery, 150 miles. 11. Atlanta to Savannah, 270 miles. 12. Macon to Albany, 100 miles. 13. Talladega to Selma, 90 miles. 14. Augusta to Savannah, 120 miles.

Running in a direction from east to west, we find—1. Memphis to Chattanooga. 2. Vicksburg to Jackson, to Marion, 130 miles. 3. Marion to Cahawba, 90 miles. 4. Water communication from Cahawba to Montgomery, 70 miles. 5. Montgomery to Augusta, 300 miles. 6. Montgomery to Savannah, 360 miles. 7. Savannah to Chattahoochee, 300 miles. 8. Savannah to Tallahassee, 240 miles.

9. Brunswick to Waresborough, 60 miles. 10. Jacksonville to Tallahassee, 170 miles. 11. Jacksonville to Cedar Keys, 120 miles.

A great number of turnpikes and other roads exist, passing through the country in all directions, and permitting movement of troops, as well from north to south as from east to west.

This zone has a great extent of coast. Possessing a number of bays and sounds, it is therefore admirably suited for combined naval and military operations. In mentioning the rivers, we have named the most important of these bays and sounds. Be it, however, remarked that most of the bays in the Gulf of Mexico are shallow, with sandy banks, and do not admit vessels of great draught.

**Movement of Troops in the Lower Center Zone.**—Considering this as a theater of war by itself—and it is large enough for that—we may, as we did before, subdivide it into right, left, and center. But here the question arises, are we to place ourselves on the Savannah as a base of operation, or on the Tennessee? In the first case, the region along the Tennessee would form the right, the coast district the left, and the country between the two the center zone.

Taking the Tennessee for our base, the State of Mississippi would form the right, Alabama the center, and Georgia the left. The marching of troops in the three last zones from north to south would probably not find very great difficulties. The troops might, in most cases, follow the course of the rivers; besides, simultaneously with a march from north to south, gun-boats of light draught might penetrate the rivers, and establish communications with the sea, thereby facilitating the provisioning of the army, and at the same time the passage of the river.

The right zone seems particularly favorable for such operations, considering that the Memphis and New Orleans, and the Corinth and New Orleans Railroad, the Mississippi, and the Tombigbee may serve as so many lines of communication with the base on the Tennessee or the Ohio, as well as with the sea.

But the center zone also offers facilities. Good roads exist from Decatur to Columbia, a distance of only one hundred miles, or six days' march; thence to Pensacola is railroad communication, and to Mobile water communication.

Operating at the extreme right, though it would perhaps be greatly facilitated by a flotilla in the Mississippi, might encounter difficulties in the number of the tributaries of the Mississippi which would have to be crossed. Operating at the extreme left would be difficult, in consequence of the swampy condition of the country.

It should be remarked, however, that little would be gained by marching simply from north to south in this zone, considering its length and width—from the Upper Savannah to the Mississippi about four hundred miles, and from the Lower Savannah to the Mississippi about six hundred miles—an army, after having marched south a certain distance, would then have to march east or west, and would find itself in the same position as an army taking the Savannah as a base of operations.

An army marching from the Savannah to the west, might march in the neighborhood of the Tennessee; or, at all events, as far north as possible. The nearer the Tennessee, the easier, probably, the movement. What renders a movement from east to west, or west to east, difficult in this zone, is the number of large rivers which an army would have to cross. The nearer to the springs of these rivers, therefore, the movement takes place, the easier it will be executed. An operation to the left—that is, near the sea-coast—would only be possible when supported by a large flotilla; and even then it would be slow, and productive of small results.

Operating in the center zone would offer as many difficulties as operating in the left. In marching, therefore, from east to west, an army could only act to the right—that is, near the Tennessee—or, perhaps, take a slanting direction, starting from the extreme right, and marching diagonally through the country—from Pickens, for instance, in the direction of New Orleans. Thus, only a comparatively small number of rivers would have to be passed; and, besides, the distance is reduced, and communication might soon be opened with the sea as well as with the center of the base of operation—that is, the Savannah near Augusta.

The **Right Zone** consists of the country west of the Mississippi, and is formed mainly by the States of Missouri, Arkansas, and Louisiana. The main feature of this zone is the great abundance of rivers. A mountain chain runs from north to south, parallel to the Mississippi, from Helena, near this river, up into Missouri. It is called Crowley's Ridge. The country between this ridge and the Mississippi is almost one large swamp. In fact, the abundance of water in this zone creates a great number of swamps.

The principal direction of the course of the rivers is from northwest to southeast. They are all the tributaries or confluents of the Mississippi. This zone being of comparatively little importance, we give only the principal features of it without many details.

The principal rivers are—

1. The *Missouri River*. 2. The *Francis River*. 3. The *White River*. 4. The *Arkansas River*. 5. The *Red River*.

An immense number of smaller rivers, or confluents of the above named, or emptying direct into the Mississippi, traverse the country in all directions. The lower portions of this zone — Arkansas and Louisiana — are unhealthy, in consequence of the many swamps. Its extent, from north to south, is about seven hundred miles; and from east to west, from two hundred and fifty to three hundred miles.

The principal towns are—

**In Missouri.**—St. Louis, Jefferson City, Hannibal, Palmyra, St. Charles, Booneville, Lexington, and Bloomington.

**In Arkansas.**—Little Rock and Van Buren.

**In Louisiana.**—Barataria, Bayou Sara, Carrollton. New Orleans and Baton Rouge, though in Louisiana, belong, in fact, to the center zone.

The principal lines of communication, besides the Mississippi, Missouri, Arkansas, and Red Rivers, are the railroads from—1. Hannibal to St. Joseph. 2. Hudson to St. Charles. 3. St. Louis to Georgetown, from east to west. 4. St. Louis to Wynesville, from east to west. 5. St. Louis to Pilot Knob, from north to south. 6. Memphis to Little

Rock, only partly finished. 7. Vicksburg to Marshall, in Texas, not entirely finished. 8. New Orleans to Franklin.

This zone possesses some continuous and parallel roads, from Missouri south to Louisiana; and also a number of roads from east to west. An army operating in it would have to contend with many obstacles. In Arkansas, a large army, even if only on a rapid march through, would probably find difficulties in obtaining subsistence. In marching from north to south, it would have to cross a great number of rivers, which afford many lines of defense to the enemy, and render an advance against a vigilant foe nearly impossible. Only along the different navigable rivers would troops be able to move with security and ease. Missouri, however, must be excepted; it is already more populated than the other two States. Louisiana, also, is probably easier to pass through than Arkansas.

It should be observed that this zone has no large center of population, or large arsenals or manufactories. Moreover, the total population being small, it will be seen that no large army can maintain itself for any length of time in this zone, unless based on the Mississippi or some of the other navigable streams, by which it could be fully supplied from the North, or any other place. In other words, a large Rebel army, thrown into this zone, having no longer control over the Mississippi or center zone, could probably not subsist for a long period of time; or, at all events, it could not carry out any campaign of importance. It would be obliged to disperse.

Having thus passed in review the different zones of which the whole theater of war is composed, there remain but a few words to say as to the connection of those zones with each other.

The left zone and the upper center zone are contiguous. They are linked together by the mountain chain. However, the communications are comparatively few. East Tennessee and Virginia, and the Charleston and Chattanooga Railroad, and a restricted number of turnpikes or ordinary roads, are all that join East Kentucky and Tennessee with Virginia and North and South Carolina.

The communications between the left and lower center zone are better. The Charleston and Augusta, and the Charleston and Savannah Railroads, besides the river, may be crossed at a great number of points.

The communication between the northern and southern center zone is across the Tennessee. The party commanding the river may cross at any point from one zone into the other. Chattanooga forms on the Tennessee a kind of *tête-de-pont;* besides which, some roads over the mountains exist, joining North Georgia with East Tennessee and Kentucky.

The communication between the center and the right zone exists now only at Vicksburg, which thereby becomes a point of great strategic importance. The Mississippi River is much too large to be crossed in any other way than by steam-boats; but the party possessing them may cross at many points.

What has been said about the geography of the theater of war is, I believe, sufficient to enable the reader to understand well the different operations carried on in it; and which will be discussed in the following chapter.

# III.

## APPLICATION OF THE MAXIMS LAID DOWN IN CHAPTER I. TO THE THEATER OF WAR CONSTITUTED BY THE SOUTHERN CONFEDERACY.

WHATEVER be the causes of this great rebellion, we cannot but admit that, at the present moment, the war has lost all resemblance to those wars which a government has sometimes to undertake against its rebellious subjects. It has entirely assumed the character of a war carried on between two powerful neighbors. The military operations must therefore be conducted like those which have for their object the conquest and occupation of a large country possessing great and disciplined armies.

We have said above that, according as the war is national, or merely governmental as regards the invaded country, so the operations, and especially the mode of occupying the country, have to be different. In the present case, though perhaps as regards the South the war may be called national, there is no danger of such effects or results as generally attend national uprisings, because the whole male population able to bear arms is already enrolled in the regular armies, and the country, being thus stripped of its defenders, is void of all material for resistance, except where those armies happen to be. Occupation becomes, therefore, a secondary affair; and our main object should be the destruction or breaking up of the Rebel armies. This successfully accomplished, and all resistance thereby destroyed, the downfall of the Confederate government becomes a matter of course, as well as the surrender and occupation of the Southern towns and sea-ports.

Grand operations in accordance with the geography of the theater of war and those maxims which we have, in the first chapter, under the head of "Wars of Invasion," laid down as the "third system," will alone be able to bring about the destruction or breaking up of the Rebel armies, an object which, as we have just said, must be accomplished before attempting anything else.

"*Success is in the legs of the soldier,*" was a saying of Marshal Saxe; and if this be true for every kind of war, it is more especially so for great wars of conquest. Movement, continued, rapid movement, is the secret for obtaining success; and what soldiers can accomplish in that respect, may be seen in the campaigns of 1805, 1809, 1812, and 1814, etc.*

---

* In 1805 Napoleon's army was at Boulogne for the grand expedition against England, when the war with Austria broke out. Napoleon marched his army to Ulm, thence to Vienna, and thence to Austerlitz, making a total distance of 333 leagues, or 1000 miles. From Boulogne to Vienna, 900 miles, was one continuous march. In 1809 Napoleon's guard was in Spain, at Madrid and Valencia. When Napoleon was obliged to make preparations for the Austrian war, his guard marched, in nearly one continuous route, from Madrid to Vienna, a distance of not less than 666 leagues, or 2000 miles. In 1812 the army marched from the Rhine to Moscow, a distance of 600 leagues, or 1800 miles; equal to the distance between Washington and Galveston, in Texas.

The distance which the troops of Napoleon were generally obliged to march was from twenty to thirty miles a day. The distance now adopted in European armies as an ordinary day's march is seven leagues, or twenty-one miles. These rapid military operations, by which alone great successes are to be obtained, are, however, only possible when carried out on the plan that the invading army shall subsist on the country invaded.

I know that there is a great difference in this respect between this country and Europe. In Europe, at a distance of every two or three miles, thickly populated villages are to be found, where a sufficient stock of provisions is accumulated to nourish any army on its passage through. All marches are so arranged that the troops stop for the night in some village or town in which they can be quartered, and where the citizens have to lodge and feed them. No tents and camp equipage, and no provision wagons are required; and it is evident that, under these circumstances, rapid movements may be executed.

In this country, contiguous villages or towns are the exception; a number of farms may be met with, but the quartering of troops on these farms or in towns is out of the question; therefore camping remains a necessity here. But in regard to providing for the army, matters are different; the number of farms, and the stock of cattle and other provisions accumulated in them, are sufficient to provide for an army corps, if it only marches fifteen to twenty miles a day. It is probable that an army of 100,000 men, marching on *one* road only, would, with difficulty, find sufficient provisions; but marching in three or four columns, on three or four parallel roads, the thing could certainly be done. Nothing but a good administration or organization for collecting the provisions and paying for them is required. Based on such a system of living, and freed of part of its immense wagon-trains, an army in this country may march on an average from seventeen to eighteen miles with ease.

The difference between this country and Europe in the difficulties of operations becomes more marked in the wet and cold season. In Europe, operations never become impossible. The difficulties of marching may be greater in the bad season, the sanitary state of the army may be less satisfactory, still operations may be carried on; for after a march, or after rain or cold, the soldier at all events finds in the evening a dry, warm place, and something to eat. This cannot be said of operations in the wet and cold season here. After a march in the rain, wet to the skin, the soldier arrives at his camping place; no fire can be made, or is of any use, because to be near the fire is equivalent to remaining in the rain. The soldiers in this state have to pitch their small tents; for beds, they have to use the wet ground; and for supper, a wet cracker.

There are few constitutions able to resist such treatment. Marches in the snow and cold are nearly quite as bad, and it is evident that such circumstances must produce sickness and demoralization among the troops. Besides all this, the roads in bad weather very soon become impassable. One day's rain is sometimes sufficient to render useless roads which are excellent when dry. Therefore, if any regard is entertained for our armies, winter campaigns ought to be undertaken as little as possible in this country. All energetic operations should be reserved for the dry season.

Being convinced that none but grand strategic operations can finish this war in a speedy and brilliant manner, and being also convinced that these operations cannot be carried on without the adoption of a thorough and sound system of requisition, I will assume, in the following application of principles to the theater of war, that the troops have to move only under such favorable conditions.

We have seen that the theater of war is divided by natural lines into three or four zones, distinctly separated from each other, and forming, in consequence of their great extent, theaters of war by themselves. To attack these three zones at the same time with equal means, would evidently lead to a great division of force. It is also easy to see that these three zones are of very different political as well as military importance, besides being of different extent. Nothing good could therefore be expected from a plan throwing equal forces into the most and the least important of these zones. On the other hand, the armies raised to carry on this war are so large that it would be impossible to use them all in one zone. We must therefore adopt several lines of operation, and act at least in two zones simultaneously. But then we should do what Napoleon did in all his wars against Austria, where he had two lines of operation—one in Italy and one in Germany. The main force, the main effort, and the decisive operation were always made in one zone, to which all that was done in the other zone was subordinate.

In 1805 and 1809 Prince Eugene operated in Italy; but his operations were secondary to those of Napoleon in the valley of the Danube.

These secondary lines of operation are great diversions; the enemy opposes them, and engages thereby a force distant from the really decisive point. The decisive blow is struck, and those forces distantly engaged are very often unable to take any further part in the struggle, so much are they thrown out of the way.

We may, by acting in this manner, operate in the three zones simultaneously; and it remains to determine the relative importance of these three zones, and the number of troops which, according to their importance, is to be engaged in each of them.

Of the three zones, it is easy to perceive that the right one, formed by the country west of the Mississippi, is the least important. The entire population is small; the communications with the center zone are few; the country is in great part unhealthy and difficult to operate in; insufficient lines of communication; insufficient means of provisioning; few large towns containing manufactories. All these defects combined make its occupation of little value. Moreover, the distance from the two seats of government is too great. Events and news having to travel so far are stale when they arrive. Lastly, the war in the two other zones would in no way be affected by the total occupation or conquest of this zone. To operate in it requires, therefore, only a comparatively small corps, the main object being to cover the frontier of Illinois, and to keep the upper part—that is, Missouri—clear of Rebels or guerrillas.

The left zone is the very reverse of the right one. Most of the largest towns in the North are near the left zone, which itself contains the capital of the Rebels, and quite a number of their largest cities. Washington, Baltimore, and Philadelphia are contiguous or only a few days' march distant. Besides containing the seats of the two belligerent governments, this zone acquires special interest and importance from entering higher into the Northern territory than any of the other parts of the Southern Confederacy, and thereby becoming more offensive than any of the others.

The center zone is, in importance, between the two. No strategic, decisive point is there. The extent of it is very great; and operations, with a complete result, could only be carried on by very large armies. If, therefore, this zone be chosen as the main theater of the war, the government would be obliged to hold in the left zone a very large army for its own protection; an army which would become entirely useless in the campaign, as it would have only a defensive character.

There can be no doubt, therefore, that what has been said is sufficient to establish the fact that the left zone is the main zone for decisive operations, and we will endeavor to show that its geographical formation is such that it is really well adapted for carrying them out. The army operating in the center zone will be secondary to that of the left zone, and should only serve as a kind of diversion.

Comparing what has been said, under the head of "Base of Operation, fig. 1, with the left zone, we shall find that it exactly corresponds with the case stated there: *a b* would represent the Potomac; *b d*, the Atlantic Ocean; *a c*, the mountain chain, or the frontier of Western Virginia; and *c d*, the Savannah. If we succeed in placing our army along *a c*, we should be able to act or take hold at any moment of the communications of the army A, which has for its only retreat the line *c d*, or the Savannah. The very moment a Rebel army permits a Union army to act from the mountain district against its communications, or, what is better, to take hold of them, so as to force it to fight, forming its line of battle parallel with the sea, and facing the Blue Ridge—that is, forming its line of battle parallel with its natural line of retreat to the Savannah—this Rebel army, in case of defeat, will not only be beaten, but, by a rapid pursuit, will be obliged to surrender, as it will be thrown back in the direction of the ocean, an obstacle which soon stops all further retreat.

The possession of the mountain district is therefore, for the holding of the left zone, a necessity; and still better, it is a necessity for the possession of the whole theater of war. In fact, this chain of mountains is like a wedge driven from the North right into the very heart of the theater of war. It is the only elevated part of it, and dominates it in all directions. It is like a bulwark, or, better still, like the citadel of a large fortress, of which the walls are formed by the parallel ridges, the ditches by the rapid streams in the valley, and the doors by the gaps.

Take the whole fortress—that is, the whole South—but leave this citadel untouched, and it will be the same as if nothing had been taken. In these mountains the Southern armies can rally, and, as by their occupation they maintain a decidedly central position, combined with the facility of debouching in any place, they can throw themselves, with their whole force, on all the surrounding fragments of our armies, and beat them in detail.

Take this bulwark—this key of the whole Southern Confederacy—first, and the very reverse will take place. Our armies are then in the central position, and are able to throw themselves on the fragments of the Southern armies with their united forces.

The conquest of the South, after the occupation of this citadel, will not even be a matter of time. Resistance would be useless, and surrender would be the natural consequence. Ought we not be able to carry this natural fortification, with two sides backing our territory on the Potomac and Western Virginia, and with an open door like the Shenandoah valley?

Supposing, therefore—as it was at the commencement of the war, or even of 1862—that the entire theater of war was still intact, and that we had to start on the first campaign, we should act in accordance with the importance of these three zones. We should place only a small corps in the right zone; in the center zone we should concentrate a very large army, disposed near the Ohio, between Louisville and Cincinnati, and between this latter town and Burlington, at the mouth of the Big Sandy River. On the Potomac, also, we should concentrate a large army between Harper's Ferry and Washington.

We should commence operations in the right zone to attract attention there; and then we should push, at all hazards, a sufficiently strong column from Louisville in the direction of Nashville, with the positive order to carry any obstacle in its advance. As soon as this movement was in full execution, we should concentrate at Burlington, by rapid movements, the bulk of the army placed near the Ohio, and march it, by forced marches, thence along the Big Sandy River, in a straight direction, on the Chattanooga and Lynchburg Railroad, so as to hit this road near Wytheville and Liberty. At the same moment this Ohio army started, the Potomac army ought to start.

Some strong demonstrations ought to be made against Centreville, a place where we suppose the Rebel army to be, as, in fact, they were at the commencement of 1862. The right wing of the Potomac army ought to move, by forced marches, up the Shenandoah valley; and the center and left wing should do the same in the parallel valley, between Blue Ridge and Bull Run Mountains.

From Berlin, on the Potomac, to Lynchburg and Liberty is about ten days' march; and from Burlington, on the Ohio, to Liberty is about the same distance. The marches of these two armies ought to be arranged in columns similar to those employed by Napoleon in his manœuvres of 1805 and 1806. (See "Summary of the Art of War," pp. 179 and 180.)

The object of this manœuvre is to gain the left flank of the Rebel army; and it will be seen, by measuring the distance, that if the Rebel army is induced to stay one day longer after the start has commenced, in consequence of the demonstrations against its front, its left flank will be gained either immediately by the Potomac army, or somewhat later by the Ohio army, which, in fact, arrives in its rear. In both cases the Union armies must only keep pace with the retreating Rebel army, and advance direct to the south, and they will force the Rebel army to surrender near Wilmington, in consequence of the line of retreat of the Rebels end-ing there on the sea-coast, and the way westward being closed by Union forces. (See Plate II.)

The double advance of these two armies—one on the left flank and the other right against the base of operation of the Rebel army—renders all resistance in Virginia useless, and makes it even a military fault. The stopping a day to give or receive battle from the army of the Potomac, would carry the Ohio army one day's march in advance, and the ruin of the Rebel Virginia army would be certain; for it cannot afford to lose one day, as we have shown.

It must, however, be said that, in order to render this manœuvre—that is, the adoption of two lines of operation in one zone—a safe one, it is necessary that the Ohio and the Potomac armies should each be strong enough single-handed to accept battle from the whole Rebel army; and there would be no difficulty in that, considering that the Ohio army, threatening by its position the center zone, would have obliged the Rebels to keep a large army there. Moreover, the United States fleet, by making repeated attacks and descents on different points of the coast, would compel them, in order to protect their sea-coast towns, to have sufficient forces distributed along them, which would also have absorbed a large number of troops.

The instant one of the Union armies has gained the left flank of the Rebel army, the latter may be obliged at any moment to fight a battle under conditions similar to those imposed on the Prussians while at Jena—that is to say, defeat would be equivalent to destruction. On the other hand, suppose the Union army is defeated, it would lose, perhaps, a few thousand prisoners, and be thrown back on its base of operation; but the defeat would in no way be decisive, as it would be if inflicted on the Southern army.

Evidently the Rebel army would try to avoid such a catastrophe; and could only do so by retreating immediately to the Upper Savannah. The Union army, continuing to push its right wing forward, is a few days afterward reinforced by the Ohio army, and it becomes apparent that this one march along the right of the left zone will carry the whole left zone in twenty or twenty-five days, even if it does not accomplish the destruction of the Rebel army at first contained in it.

How difficult the escape of the Rebel army would be, may be imagined, when we consider the embarrassment of the enemy in understanding so grand an operation before it is fully developed, and of resolving at once upon a counter-operation equally grand, leaving, perhaps, a well-fortified position, which their adversaries, to judge from their demonstrations, seemed disposed to attack. The difficulty for the Rebel commander would be to distinguish, amid the noise of battle, in the continually succeeding news and dispatches, the true from the false. Melas, Mack, and the Duke of Brunswick, all three in their day, showed that the task was above their strength.

After the junction of the two armies, they would march on, always along the right of the left zone, one of the two holding the mountains—that is to say, moving along the valleys. By considering, now, the upper center zone, it will be seen that this same march which carries the left zone, carries also the upper center zone. In fact, of this zone, which nearly forms a quadrangle, the Rebels hold, or did hold, only one side, and this is the side extending from Florence to Lynchburg.

The Lower Cumberland and Tennessee could always be passed by Union gun-boats, and a retreat by the Rebels against the lower part of these two rivers would be impossible. Nor could the Ohio and the Big Sandy Rivers serve as lines of retreat. A Rebel army in Kentucky or Tennessee, in order to retreat, must therefore pass south, between Nashville and Cumberland Gap. This last side of the quadrangle the Union army is closing by its advance along the valleys.

We have said that the small army pushed, by way of diversion, from Louisville in the direction of Nashville, should advance at all hazards. This force should attack the main Rebel army in Tennessee, having orders to fight any Rebel force it might encounter. It would attack this army and be beaten. The Rebels would probably pursue it, which would carry them farther north—that is to say, away from the decisive point, or only opening left for this retreat, and which the Union army is about to close.

In this zone it would therefore be, as in the left, one day lost might witness the destruction of the whole Rebel force of Kentucky and Tennessee. If the Rebel army has not fallen back into Alabama before the Union army arrives at Chattanooga, it will be forced to fight a battle, facing southward, against superior numbers; and in case of defeat, it will be thrown against the Ohio or Lower Cumberland, where it would finally be obliged to lay down its arms.

By measuring the distance, it will be found that if the Rebels would arrive before Louisville when the Ohio army arrives at Liberty, or, better still, Wytheville, on the Lynchburg and Chattanooga Railroad, this latter army can prevent their returning into Alabama. The defeat of the secondary Union force left in Tennessee would thereby have occasioned the destruction of the Rebels.

Plate II. will better explain the movement than all that can be said about it. The same time—that is to say, twenty to twenty-five days from the first start—would therefore have sufficed to clear also the upper center zone entirely of the enemy's army. There remain but the operations against the lower center and against the right zone.

The Union armies having arrived at the north of Georgia, and occupying the table-land commanding the whole of the lower center zone, would have to commence operations against it; but here matters would be very different, according to the previous successes of the two Union armies. If they should have succeeded in destroying one, or even both Rebel armies, or in crippling them seriously, no difficulty would be experienced in the lower center zone; but if both Rebel armies—that is, that of Kentucky and that of Virginia—should have succeeded in escaping intact, the matter becomes very serious.

The best that could be expected, in the latter case, is a campaign like the second half of the campaign of 1809, with its bloody battles of Essling and Wagram; and the worst that might take place would be like that of 1812, with its disasters of Krasnoi and the Beresina. Both these two campaigns or invasions were based on the same principle as that we are discussing. In the first, the enemy's army was only partly crippled at the onset; in the second, it remained intact.

If the Rebel armiy should have been seriously crippled or partly destroyed in the previous operation, its resistance in the lower center zone could only be of short duration and without result. In fact, these retreating fragments of Rebel armies could only go in the direction of Florida or of the Mississippi. In the first case, the best thing to do would be to push them right into Florida, and to let them perish there. In the second case, one part of the Union army would follow the retreating Rebel army in the rear, the other and larger part following on the flank by advancing always in the more northerly region of the lower center zone. All rivers which would serve as lines of defense against the army following in the rear are carried, or, better, turned by the army advancing on the flank; and however strong a position of defense the Rebels would have chosen, it would always be untenable, on account of being continually outflanked. This army then would be obliged to cross the Mississippi, and once in the right zone, the war might be considered as virtually ended.

But if, on the contrary, the Rebel armies should have escaped intact our rapid manœuvres, they would be able to unite and to form a body of great strength. The Union armies, in their rapid advance, have been greatly diminished. Stragglers and sick have thinned their ranks; a number of detachments, to occupy important towns, to secure and establish communications with the sea, have made a still larger reduction; and if these two armies have started with a grand total of 400,000 men, their ultimate number, after their three weeks' campaign, would probably not exceed 250,000 men, if even this number could be brought together. The Rebels, on the contrary, by taking up every detachment, by uniting all fractions, might bring together a much larger force; and if at this moment the Union army, animated by its previous successes, were to go headlong against the united Rebel army, the result might be a complete disaster, as no fresh base of operation, and no new plan of refuge would have been secured. A pursuit over a line of from 500 to 600 miles would ruin any regular army, still more so a volunteer one; besides, most of the detachments which have been made would be lost.

The Union army should therefore come to a halt, to take breath and to establish a new base of operation, or even two; one along the Savannah, and one along the Tennessee. Gun-boats should enter the Savannah River, and command it as far as Augusta. This latter town should be partly fortified to form a secure *tête-de-pont*. The passages over the Tennessee River should be secured, *têtes-de-pont* established, the railroad lines to the north reopened, and, finally, stragglers and reinforcements brought in to replenish the army. Then operations may be recommenced. The plan would be the same here, where the united Union forces would have to contend with the united Rebel armies, as in the left zone, viz., to throw the Rebels back upon the sea. In a campaign of this description, in which good generals would be opposed to each other, as might be concluded from the previous movements of both parties, all would depend on who makes the first fault. However, the final result, if the two temporary bases of operation are well secured, cannot be dubious. The superiority of numbers would be with the North; and each of the three States would fall, one after the other—Georgia first; then, taking the Chattahoochee as a fresh temporary base of operation, Alabama could be carried up to the Tombigbee, which river, in its turn, would serve as a base of operation against Mississippi.

That the whole campaign we have here laid down is really a correct application of the rules of strategy to the geography of the theater of war, may be easily verified by recapitulating them:—

1. The principle of engaging the main force on the decisive point has been strictly followed. Two large armies, two-thirds or more of the whole disposable force, were united for the purpose of operating in one zone, which was at the same time the decisive one.

2. The plan of the threatening of many and distant points in the first disposition, and the formation of interior lines by uniting quickly the different army corps, has also found its application. The army of the Ohio threatened the whole upper center zone; its rapid movement to the east brought it to a junction with the Potomac army, with which it held interior lines, or a central position against the Rebel forces in Virginia and Kentucky.

3. The formation of two lines of operation in one zone was necessitated and according to rules. It forced the enemy also to the adoption of two lines, or a division of force; besides, it would have been impossible to move the whole army on one line; and as each of the two Union armies was superior to the Rebel army both had to deal with, and as, at the same time, the lines of operation con-

ducted to a junction beyond the reach of the enemy, the application of the principle must be considered safe and justifiable.

4. The strategic direction of the line of operation, or the choice of the base of operation for the left zone, was such that the enemy was forced to retreat, to leave an immense territory in the hands of our armies, or to fight a battle in which defeat was for him equivalent to destruction; whereas defeat for us meant nothing more than the sacrifice of a few thousand men and the loss of time—therefore the choice of the line of operation was decisive against the enemy, but not against us.

5. Finally, the strategic direction of the line of operation in reference to the entire theater of war was such that it conducted us right into the heart of the theater of war; dividing the Rebel forces continually, and always holding a crushing superiority in a central position.

In comparing this imaginary campaign with that of 1800, devised by Napoleon for the invasion of Italy and Germany, it will be found that the mountain region passing through the South plays the same rôle in the former as Switzerland did in the latter. By advancing to Shaffhausen, and there crossing the Rhine, and by entering Italy through the Alps, of which he held the gaps, Napoleon took, in the rear, the lines of Kray and Melas, in the valleys of the Danube and the Po. The left zone would be, in our theater of war, what the valley of the Danube was, and Kentucky and Tennessee what the valley of the Po was in the campaign of 1800.

It is evident that such operations, aimed right at the destruction of the enemy's armies, are decisive; that all towns, sea-ports, etc. fall as a matter of course; and that, applied to the South, from two to two and a half months would be all that should be required to carry them through.

However, against every attack there is a defense, and there are several in the present case. Nearly all brilliant manœuvres or successes in war are based on a blunder of the enemy; on a slight fault in his position; on a slight deficiency in his vigilance; neglect in the transmission of dispatches; on the dull comprehension of a general; on his natural slowness or rashness, etc.

Operations which might be undertaken with brilliant success against mediocre generals, would turn out disasters if conducted against a master of his art. Therefore, supposing that at the outset of the campaign the left flank of the Rebels could have been gained, is supposing that their first position was faulty, as in fact it was on the plains of Manassas or Centreville; it is supposing that they lost time, one or even two days, after the movement on the Upper Potomac had begun, before they commenced their retrograde movement; it is supposing that they did not understand at once the meaning of the whole movement; that they had not studied their theater of war, nor the rules of strategy; it is supposing many things more, which, after the proof of their abilities that they gave us in 1862, we are not permitted to suppose any longer.

The plan of defense worthy of the plan of attack, would have been to dispose a large reserve army along the railroad, between Chattanooga and Lynchburg; to send out from this great concentrated force two smaller armies, like two feelers, one in the direction of Louisville or Cincinnati, the other in the direction of Thoroughfare Gap. At the first movement of the Potomac or Ohio army, these two armies retreat, closely defending, step for step, and forming, finally, a junction with the main Rebel force. This main army throws itself between the two Union armies, and, from its central position, tries to defeat first one and then the other.

The Union armies, in this case, should have followed a similar course to that pursued by the allied armies in 1813, in Saxony, acting on exterior lines against Napoleon, who was forming interior lines. They always refused battle when the main army under Napoleon advanced against them, but advanced boldly the very moment this army had left and nothing but the army of observation remained opposed to them. They thereby so closely approached and wearied the army on the interior lines, by the numerous counter-marches necessary, that at the battle of Leipsic those three armies, acting on exterior lines, arrived in time, and took part in the fight.

In this first case of defense, we have supposed that the Rebels acted strictly on correct principles; that, from the simple concentration of our troops, they guessed at once the whole plan of operations, and took the necessary steps to prevent its execution.

Had they not been so circumspect—that is, had they been surprised in the first moment—but then, as soon as they understood the movement, taken the necessary steps to prevent disasters, their defense would have presented another aspect. Their first care would have been to reach intact the Upper Savannah with one army, and Cumberland Gap and Knox-

Fig. 5.

Richmond
City Point
Petersburg
James River
Chesterfield C.H.
Appomattox River
Chula

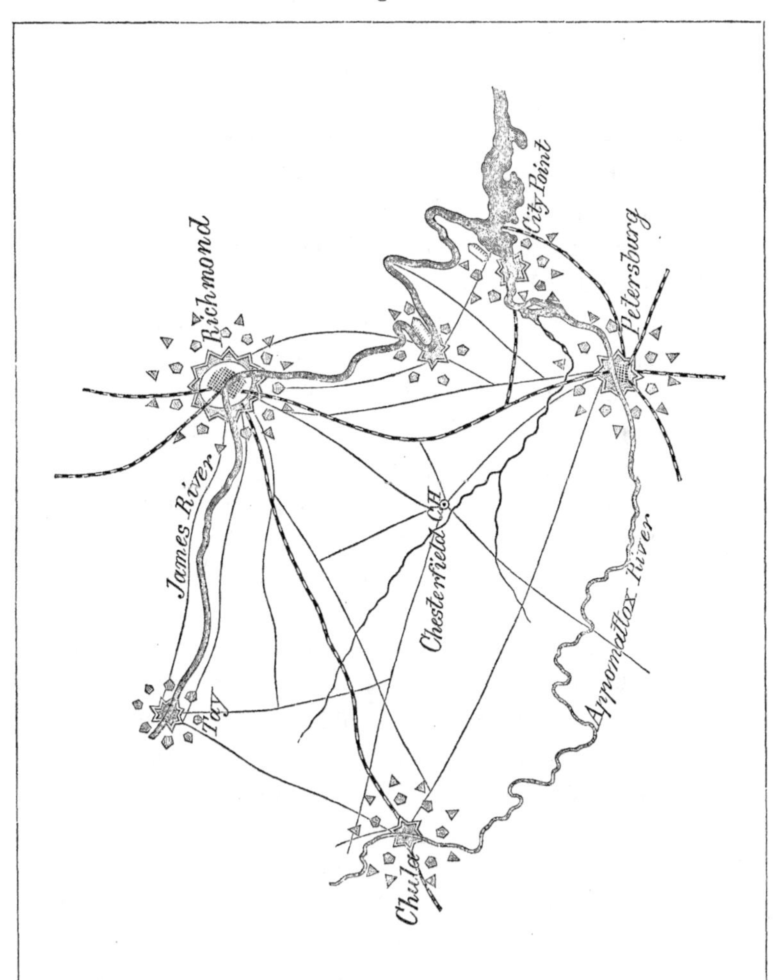

ville with the other, in order to form in those localities a junction of all their disposable forces, and to act as we have already described above, when speaking of the attack in case the Rebel armies escaped. It need be further remarked only, that the Rebels should, after this, try to hold the table-land of North Georgia; should try to prevent the establishing of temporary but secure bases of operation, on the Savannah and Tennessee, by our troops; or should give these latter no time to obtain reinforcements, etc.

The third and last mode of defense, and for a small force perhaps the surest of success, would be a system of fortifications and of *têtes-de-pont* round Richmond. Such a system would quickly put a stop to all rapid operations; it would prolong the war, and, perhaps, baffle the greatest exertions of the attacking forces.

The James and Appomattox Rivers offer extensive facilities for the adoption of a similar plan. Fig. 5 will show which of the places on those rivers would be the most advantageous to fortify. These fortifications would form a system similar to the Austrian quadrilateral in Italy. It might be objected that for the defense of works sò extensive, a great number of men would be required; and that these being taken from the army, would diminish its efficiency. This is, to a certain extent, true; but here, as in all similar cases, probably convalescents, recruits, or men too old for active service, but not for the defense of a fortification, would be made use of.

The main fortifications, as they all form *têtes-de-pont*, should be strong; the guns in embrasures, and not *en barbette;* the *corps-de-place* should be surrounded by a number of forts flanking each other, and able to contain, camped between them, a large army. The system of fortification, in one word, should be what is called the German system.

Supposing now that both sides of Richmond, as well as Petersburg, were fortified in this way, both forming double *têtes-de-pont* and large camps, with a similar system of fortification existing on the Appomattox, just above City Point, and that this was joined to one on the James River, above City Point, as shown in the figure; that, finally, similar works existed above Richmond, between Goochland C. H. and the latter town, as well as on the Appomattox, where the Richmond and Lynchburg Road crosses it. Supposing all these works existing, and certainly part of them do already exist, a large Rebel army might take shelter at any moment in the middle of them; and by basing itself now on one, now on the other of the fortifications, it could take any position, any front, without any possibility of being cut from its base.

The defense of the fortifications should be conducted like that of Sebastopol—that is, aggressive in itself to a certain extent—and the field army should not leave the attacking or invading army one instant in repose. The time the Rebels would gain by a similar defense should be employed in the concentration of their entire force, so as to drive the Union army back.

It should also be remarked that this system would force the Union army to leave the advantageous direction of its line of operation, and to base itself on the James or Pamunkey Rivers, which is equivalent to giving up all decisive operations in the main left zone. The formation of a fortified double *tête-de-pont* at Lynchburg might perhaps also prove an advantage.

It would be impossible to discuss here the operations which might take place in consequence of such a system of defense; we may remark that they might be brilliant, and some of them, perhaps, entirely new. What can be done, under similar circumstances, is shown by Radetzky's manœuvres, in 1848, in the Austrian quadrilaterals.

Before closing this chapter, I wish to repeat once more, that the whole of the above reasoning is only based on such a knowledge of the theater of war as I could derive from common maps. There may be several mistakes in the geography, or in the application of the principles laid down to a geography which is not correct. The reader, in this case, must be indulgent, and only consider that what has been said is already more than sufficient to show, in its general form, the application of the rules of grand war to the theater of operations formed by the Southern Confederacy.

We will now pass on to the campaign of 1862.

# IV.

## CAMPAIGN OF 1862.

Before entering on the discussion of this campaign, I will give a short and simple narrative of it. I have no other sources of information at my disposal than the accounts published by the press of the country, and hence some of the details, as well as some of the dates and figures, may have been incorrectly stated.

The reader must excuse such mistakes, if there are any; the more so, as the description of the campaign is not intended for a history, but merely for the text of a strictly military criticism. Besides, I design merely to discuss the great movements, and not to enter into details of battles or of smaller operations. It will therefore be of little or no importance if some of the petty details should have been omitted or inaccurately set down.

To render the discussion more easily understood, and to give a view of the whole of the past campaign, I have added a map on which will be found the positions of the armies, and the principal lines of operation of these armies during the campaign of 1862.

The year 1861 had closed with enormous preparations for this campaign. With recruiting, manufacturing of arms, organizing regiments and armies, the latter months of 1861 had passed away; and the new year found an immense army and navy, created from almost nothing, ready to take the field. The fear of foreign intervention, called forth by the Trent affair, had subsided; and we find the principal actors in the great drama everywhere engaged in giving the last touches to the vast preparations and armaments just ready to be launched against the Southern Confederacy.

The fleet had taken the advance of the army, and was already fully engaged in accomplishing its part in the great struggle. The blockade and shutting up of the Southern harbors was in full operation at the beginning of 1862. Up to the middle of January nothing of importance took place. Skirmishing, reconnoitering, and foraging were the order of the day, until the 12th of January, when the campaign was really opened by the starting of General Burnside, with four brigades, numerous transports, and gun-boats, from Fortress Monroe for an unknown destination.

In the West this start was soon followed; concentration of troops had taken place in Missouri, in Illinois, near Cairo, and in North Kentucky, on the Louisville and Nashville Railroad. Numerous iron-clad river gun-boats had been constructed to act on the Mississippi, Ohio, and Tennessee, etc. On the 19th of January the first clang of battle was heard in the West, and the first Union victory was gained by General Thomas over General Zollikoffer, at Mill Springs, near Somerset, Ky.

The river navy, determined not to be behindhand with the army, in its turn commences with a brilliant exploit. Flag-officer Foote captures Fort Henry, on the Tennessee River, on the 6th of February, which fort was designed to close this river to any Union advance; and he then ascended the river as far as Florence.

In Missouri, the Union army, under General Curtis, advances against Springfield, a position held by the Rebel General Price; another army, under General Pope, nears New Madrid; General Grant advances with his troops in the direction of Fort Donelson, along the peninsula formed by the Cumberland and the Tennessee Rivers; General Buell pushes forward to encounter the Rebels at Bowling Green; and smaller corps advance in the direction of Cumberland Gap.

The whole West, over a distance of 600 miles, is in motion, and the motto is everywhere "forward." Fort Donelson, situated on the Cumberland River, below Dover, is attacked by General Grant's army, and, after a severe fight, and the escape of part of its garrison, it surrenders, on the 16th of February, leaving 12,000 to 15,000 prisoners and immense quantities of material of war in the hands of the victors.

Pressed in front by General Buell, outflanked by the gunboats, and General Grant's army ascending the Cumberland and the Tennessee Rivers, the Rebel troops in Kentucky begin to fear for their communications; they evacuate Bowling Green, Clarksville, and even Nashville, taking position at Murfreesborough, under General Johnston, about twenty miles south of Nashville, which latter town is occupied by General Buell and his army on the 24th.

General Grant proceeds to Savannah, on the Tennessee River; the evacuation of Columbus, one of the strongest barriers to the passage of the Mississippi, becomes a necessity for the Rebels, if they do not wish to see their communications endangered. They accordingly retreat to Jackson, Tenn., on the 3d of March, where they form a junction with the troops already assembled under General Beauregard.

New Madrid and Island No. 10 were the only obstruc-'ons left in the great river; but they soon fall. New Madrid is evacuated by the Confederates, and occupied by General Pope's troops on the 13th of March; and Island No. 10 surrenders to the same, after a long bombardment, on the 7th of April. With it, the last barrier of the Upper Mississippi is thrown down, and the higher part of this river is reopened to Northern navigation.

In Missouri, in the mean time, events had occurred too; ice receded before the advancing Union force into Ar-ısas; Springfield is occupied by Federal troops, who ›n follow the Rebel general along the road to Fayette-ie. But Price, being reinforced by Arkansas and Texas roops, and a body of Indians 5000 to 6000 strong, forming a total of about 30,000 men, the whole under the command of General Van Dorn, does not remain any longer on the defensive, and advances from Fayetteville to encounter the Federal army under General Curtis, numbering from 0,000 to 40,000 men.

General Curtis is apprised of the advance of the Rebels, nd concentrates his force at Pea Ridge, near Sugar Creek. he Rebels, on their march to this latter place, leave the ıin road from Fayetteville to their right, and having ined the same latitude as the Union army, they move to e east, and thereby turn the position of the latter. They form their line of battle in the rear of the Federal troops, and force them to face northeast in the engagement which ensued. On the 8th of March the battle is fought, and, after a severe struggle, the Rebels are dislodged and obliged to retreat, in consequence of a flank movement executed by General Sigel. They manage, however, to escape, though our army was on their line of retreat.

General Grant, in Tennessee, had moved his army to the left bank of the Tennessee River, and encamped at Shiloh, near Pittsburg Landing. His force consisted of six divisions, namely, Hurlbut, Prentiss, Sherman, McClernand, Smith, and Wallace's. General Beauregard, meanwhile, being joined by the troops coming from Columbus, under General Polk, and by a corps coming from Mobile, under General Bragg, took a position near Corinth; and concluded, with General Johnston at Murfreesborough, an arrangement, according to which they were to form a junction of all their forces, and defeat General Grant before he could be succored by General Buell from Nashville.

This plan was put in execution by means of the Charleston and Memphis Railroad. Several unexpected incidents, so frequent in war, besides bad weather, obliged the Rebel leaders to postpone their attack for two or three days. General Buell, meanwhile, was moving from Nashville toward Shiloh, to form, in his turn, a junction with General Grant. Finally, on the 6th of April, the battle took place. General Grant's troops were somewhat taken by surprise; they rallied, however, very quickly, and were, only after a resistance lasting nearly the whole day, and attended with very heavy loss, obliged to seek shelter under their gunboats.

The different delays in the attack had given General Buell time to arrive; not, however, early enough to gain the battle fought on the 6th, but another battle, which was to be fought on the 7th. After a very severe engagement, the Rebels were finally obliged to fall back, which they did slowly and in good order, the loss and exhaustion on both sides being such that no immediate pursuit took place. The loss of the Rebels is stated to have been about 10,000; that of the Union forces was heavier, including several thousand prisoners.

General Beauregard retreated to Corinth, where he took up a fortified position. To fight the army under his command, a junction of the different Union armies, commanded by Generals Pope, Grant, and Buell, became necessary, and was also effected under the command-in-chief of General Halleck. This large Union army slowly advanced against Corinth, of which place a kind of siege was undertaken; but scarcely were the preparations for a determined attack completed, when, on the 30th of May, the Rebels disappeared, leaving their intrenchments in the hands of the Union troops. They retreated toward Grenada, at which place they took up another position unmolested by the Federal army.

The occupation of Corinth, Memphis, and all the territory between the Mississippi and Tennessee was the consequence of this retrograde movement. The occupation of Memphis was hastened by gun-boat operations on the Mississippi. Several naval engagements had taken place between Federal and Confederate gun-boats, when, on the 27th of April, Flag-officer Farragut commenced the bombardment of Forts Jackson and St. Philip, below New Orleans, on the Lower Mississippi, and, by passing above these forts, forced the City of New Orleans to surrender on the 28th of April. The next day the forts followed the example of the city, and hauled down their colors.

After the occupation of Memphis, which took place in June, only one obstruction to the navigation of the Mississippi remained, and this was Vicksburg. Great activity reigned on the river; gun-boats ascended its different affluents searching for Rebel steamers, cutting off the communications of the Rebel armies, and exploring the country.

Vicksburg also was attacked by the fleet, but resisted all attempts to capture it; and, after a bombardment lasting over a month, the siege was raised on the 25th of July. After the raising of this siege, nothing of importance took place in the West up to the invasion of Kentucky by Bragg. A few attacks by small bands were made on the Union forces at Baton Rouge, Murfreesborough, and several other places; raids were executed by Rebel cavalry or guerrillas in the interior of the already occupied territory of Missouri, Tennessee, and Kentucky, and these kept the Union troops alive.

The only incident worth mentioning is the retreat of General Curtis, who had, after the battle of Pea Ridge, penetrated into Arkansas, but found himself obliged to fall back, and was followed by the Rebel Generals Hindman and Rains. He reached Helena, on the Mississippi, on the 6th of July, and with it safety.

Such were the events of the Western campaign, which, at least at its outset, may certainly be called brilliant. Everywhere the stars and bars had given way before the old flag.

In the East, at the beginning, matters were progressing quite as satisfactorily.

General Burnside, as we have seen, sailed on the 12th of January from Fortress Monroe. He arrived on the 17th at Cape Hatteras, N. C. On the 8th of February, he attacked Roanoke Island, which surrendered after a sharp fight, leaving 3000 prisoners in the hands of the victors. From this point, as a base of operation, a number of expeditions are undertaken up the different rivers emptying into Pamlico or Albemarle Sound. On the 20th, Winton, on the Chowan River, is taken; on the 14th of March, a fight takes place at Newbern, on the Neuse River; on the 21st, Washington, on Pamlico River, is occupied; and on the 23d, Morehead is entered by General Parks's troops.

Not less fruitful of success is the more Southern theater of war in the beginning of the campaign. The force at Port Royal, S. C., placed under the command of General Hunter, attacked Fort Pulaski, which, after a bombardment, surrendered to the batteries on Tybee Island on the 11th of April. Jacksonville, and, somewhat later, also Pensacola, both in Florida, are occupied by Union troops. An attack on Charleston, on the 19th of June, however, fails, in consequence of a fight on James Island, where the Federal troops were repulsed with loss. Soon after this event, part of the troops in this section, consisting of General Stevens's division, were embarked, and sailed for Fortress Monroe, where they arrived on the 17th of July.

During the time when the events described above were transpiring in the West and the South, the army of the Potomac, under General McClellan, was not idle. On the

7th of February, Romney, in Western Virginia, is entered by the Federal troops under General Lander; and on the 24th of the same month, operations commence in the Shenandoah valley, with the occupation of Harper's Ferry by General Banks. Charlestown, Martinsburg, and Bunker Hill are occupied a few days later. On the 8th of March, Col. Geary moves from Lovettsville to Leesburg; and on the 12th, General Banks enters Winchester and Berryville.

These movements on their left flank, determine the Rebels to abandon their fortified positions at Centreville and Manassas, which places are entered by the Union troops on the 10th and 12th. From these two places, cavalry is pushed forward in the direction of Aquia Creek and Warrenton; they find the Rebels on the Rappahannock; Warrenton is still held by their cavalry.

In the Shenandoah valley, the forward movement is continued. After fighting a battle at Winchester with the Rebels under General Jackson, in which the latter were repulsed, the Federal troops enter Strasburg on the 23d of March, and Woodstock on the 1st of April. On the 17th of March, another great movement was undertaken; the embarkation of the main body of the army of the Potomac for Fortress Monroe was commenced at Alexandria.

This movement was being executed, when at Fortress Monroe, and in fact in the whole country, the greatest excitement existed in consequence of the appearance of the Rebel steamer Merrimac in Hampton Roads. On the 8th of March, this vessel, a large, old steam-frigate, which had only been half destroyed when the Union authorities left Norfolk at the outbreak of the rebellion, came out of Norfolk harbor transformed into an iron-clad war vessel. She entered Hampton Roads, and pursued a course directly toward two United States frigates—the Cumberland and the Congress—anchored at the entrance of the James River. Without heeding the shower of bullets sent against her from the two frigates, she runs into the Cumberland and sinks her. The Congress, in her turn, is attacked, and, after a short, heavy, gun action, takes fire and hauls down her colors.

In the evening of this eventful day, the Monitor, an iron-clad steamer of the North, but of a different construction from that of the Merrimac, arrives in Hampton Roads; and the next morning, when the Merrimac returns to complete her work of destruction, she finds, at least, an adversary worthy of her. After a long fight, in which neither of the two vessels gained a decisive advantage over the other, the Merrimac re-enters Norfolk harbor, and leaves the battle-field to her adversary.

Great preparations were then made at Fortress Monroe for the reception of the Rebel steamer Merrimac, should she appear once more; but she did not come. Her presence, however, rendered all operations on the James River impossible up to the moment of the evacuation of Norfolk by the Rebels, and her subsequent destruction.

In the midst of the activity and excitement created by the Merrimac at Fortress Monroe, the army of the Potomac began to arrive. It took from the 17th of March to the 4th of April to transport the larger part of the army, which numbered from 80,000 to 100,000 men, to its place of destination.

On the 5th of April, preparations had so far advanced as

to permit of a forward movement. General McClellan had arrived, and the troops were put in motion in the direction of Yorktown. General Keyes, with three divisions, formed the left, and advanced on the road to Lee's Mill. General McClellan, with the remainder of the troops, marched to the right. On the 7th, the army arrived in the neighborhood of Yorktown, and found itself in front of a long range of field-works, extending from York to James River, and occupied by a Rebel army under the orders of General Magruder.

Most of the field-works were nearly unapproachable, in consequence of the swampy condition of the ground in front. An attempt near Lee's Mill to carry them failed. The navy, trying to invest Yorktown by water, found it so well armed and provided that the object could not be effected. General McDowell, who was expected to join the army at Yorktown, to disembark near Gloucester, and, by ascending York River, to turn the Rebel position on the Peninsula, did not come, in consequence of an order of the War Department, giving him an independent command between Blue Ridge and the Potomac. Finally, James River being blockaded by the Merrimac, no alternative was left, in order to advance, but to undertake the siege of Yorktown.

Preparations for this siege were immediately made. But while the siege was going on, the troops left in the north of Virginia were not idle. They had been divided into three independent corps, of which General Fremont commanded one, in the mountains west of the Shenandoah; General Banks the next, in the Shenandoah valley; and General McDowell the third, in the country east of Blue Ridge.

On the 17th of April, Monterey, Highland County, Va., is entered by General Milroy, from Fremont's command. Mount Jackson is occupied by General Banks's troops, and the Union columns push forward to New Market and Sparta—Jackson, with his army, all the while retreating in the direction of Stannardville and Gordonsville. General McDowell, on his side, advances toward Fredericksburg; he enters Falmouth, and, on the 19th, Fredericksburg surrenders, and is occupied by the Federal troops.

Meanwhile the siege of Yorktown had proceeded; batteries had been established, and all was ready for a final blow, when, on the 4th of May, the town was reported to be evacuated by the Rebels. In fact, they had left their intrenchments, and were in full retreat toward Williamsburg. The same day, the army of the Potomac started in pursuit on two roads—one leading from Lee's Mill, the other from Yorktown to Williamsburg. On the 5th, a strong Rebel rear guard was found in position; but, after a severe engagement, was dislodged, in consequence of a successful flank movement executed by General Hancock.

While part of the army followed the Rebels by land, a body of troops, under command of General Franklin, was transported by water from Yorktown to West Point, to act on the communications of the Rebels still left on the Peninsula. This gave rise to another fight on the 7th, which the Rebels had to sustain, in order to give their troops coming from Williamsburg time to pass.

After a stay of several days at Williamsburg, the army resumed its forward movement, and arrived, on the 16th of May, at White House, on the Pamunkey River, from which point, as a temporary base, the army started, and arrived at the Chickahominy, at the place where the railroad crosses the creek, and called Bottom Bridge.

These forward movements, as well as the proximity of General Burnside, endangered the communications of the troops in and around Norfolk, the evacuation of which place consequently became a necessity; it was effected on the 12th of May, and as the town was nearly immediately afterward occupied by Union troops, the Merrimac was left without any place to go to, and was therefore blown up by its commander. The navigation on the James River being thus opened by the destruction of their powerful adversary, the Federal gun-boats immediately entered and ascended the river; but at a distance of about ten miles from Richmond, they found themselves stopped by a barrier in the river and a heavy battery at Fort Darling, both of which obstacles united rendered all efforts at further advance useless.

Between the Chickahominy Creek and Richmond, the Rebel army was encountered by the Federal troops; the Confederates were strongly intrenching themselves, rendering further immediate advance difficult. Part of the army passed the creek at Bottom Bridge; four divisions were established on the right bank, along the railroad—in echelon, one behind the other—the foremost near Fair Oaks. These divisions formed the left wing of the army; the remainder, or right wing, was established from Bottom Bridge up the creek, the higher part of which, however, remained in possession of the Rebels. (See Fig. 6.)

In this position the army remained for some time, busily engaged with establishing bridges over the creek, to secure the communication between the right and the left wing. The construction of these bridges was a difficult task, owing to the swampy condition of the river and its banks, and it took a considerable length of time. The season was exceedingly wet, and the bed of the river changed continually.

On the 26th and 27th of May, General Porter was sent to Hanover C. H., to form a junction with General McDowell. An engagement took place with a Rebel division under General Branch, in which the Federal troops remained victorious; but the projected junction was not effected—it was already too late. General McDowell, General Banks, and General Fremont, as well as the whole army forming the garrison of Washington, had been thrown on the defensive by an audacious movement of General Jackson; and the terror in and around Washington was such, that orders were even sent to burn the only bridges by which a junction between General McClellan's and General McDowell's army was possible. This is, however, how matters happened:—

On the 8th of May, Generals Jackson and Johnston, having united their forces in the Shenandoah valley, marched to attack General Milroy at Bull Pasture Mountain, Pendleton County, Va. After an engagement, General Milroy retreated to Franklin, where the remainder of General Fremont's corps was stationed. The Rebels, after some delay, marched to Front Royal, where they arrived on the 23d, and captured the small garrison, General Banks at the time being stationed, with two brigades, at Strasburg. General Jackson's force moved from Front Royal direct to Middletown, a place between Strasburg and Winchester, thereby seizing the communications of General Banks. Before, however, Jackson had arrived there in force, General Banks had commenced his retreat, and finding Middletown but feebly occupied, opened his way through, and escaped with the main body of his command. At Winchester, where a short stay was made, he was attacked by the Rebels, and, after a fight of several hours, obliged to retreat to Martinsburg, and thence across the Potomac, near Williamsport; making, in all, nearly sixty miles in two days.

General Fremont was informed of General Jackson's move on the 25th; he struck camp the same day, and marched first to Petersburg, and from there to Strasburg, where Jackson had passed but a very short time before. Nearly at the same time, the advance of General McDowell's corps arrived and joined in the pursuit. Jackson, under continual skirmishing, retreated south, and on the 7th of June it was ascertained by a reconnoissance that he had left Harrisonsburg to the right on his march, and was crossing the Shenandoah at a place called Port Republic, the only place where a bridge was to be found for a long distance.

General Fremont, who had arrived meanwhile at Harrisonsburg, on receiving this intelligence moved his army in the direction of Port Republic; but was stopped at Cross Keys, a place about half way from his destination, by the rear guard of the Rebels, about 5000 strong, drawn up in line of battle, to cover the crossing of their train and main body over the Shenandoah. General Fremont attacked their position with his 20,000 men, but without *ensemble*,

Fig. 6.

Richmond York Riv. R.R.
Chickahominy
Bottoms bridge
Swamps
Road to Malvern hill
White Oak
Summers bridge
Savage Station
U.S.
Gaines mills
Alexander bridge
C.A. 31 May
New bridge
Fair Oaks
Mechanicsville
Meadow bridge
Richmond

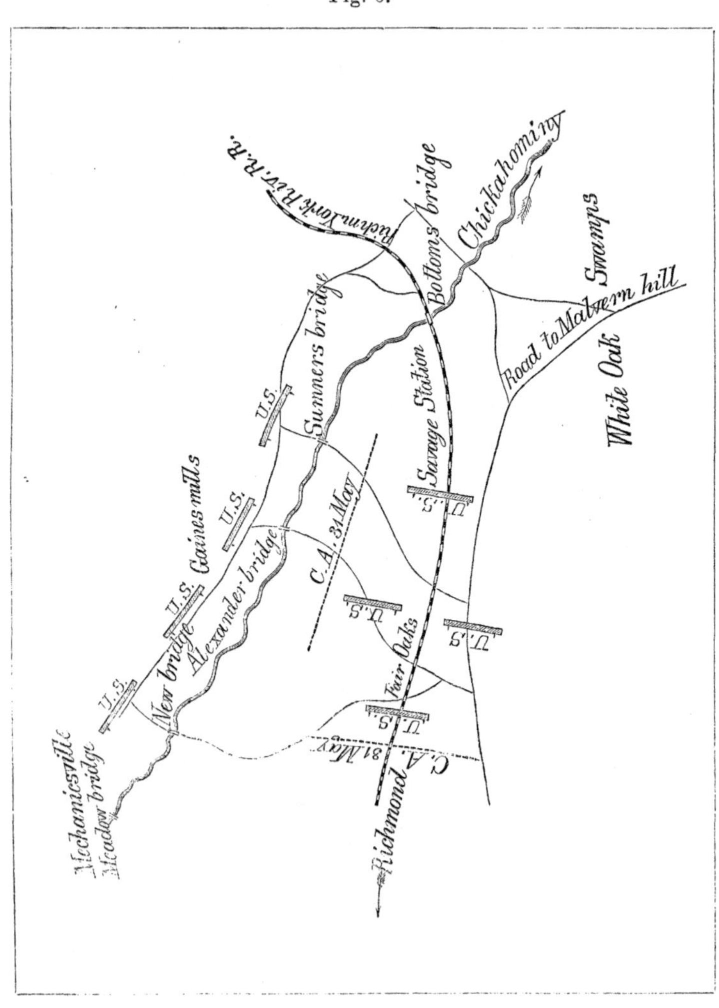

and got beaten in detail. The next morning, when revenge was to be taken for the affront of the preceding evening, the Rebel rear guard had disappeared, and was only refound on the other side of the Shenandoah; but the bridge over this river was burned.

While his rear guard was beating Fremont, Jackson, who had already crossed with his main body, found himself opposed by General Tyler, of General Shields's division, who was sent from Luray to Waynesborough, to intercept him or prevent him crossing. General Tyler paid dearly for the attempt; his brigade was nearly annihilated, and his artillery captured. General Jackson, freed from his numerous pursuers, retreated with his booty unmolested toward Gordonsville. General Shields's division belonged to General McDowell's corps, who had been ordered to join in the pursuit of Jackson, and had left Fredericksburg at the end of May.

In the mean time, while this daring movement of Jackson was taking place, the Chickahominy became the theater of more serious events. On the 31st of May and 1st of June, the battle of Fair Oaks was fought by part of the army of the Potomac. (Fig. 6.)

The Rebels, seeing the exposed position of the left wing of this army, resolved to attack it with their whole force. A thunder-storm had been raging the day before, and the rising of the Chickahominy was expected by them, and with the rising they hoped that all communications would be cut off between the right and left wings, and that the four divisions composing the left would be exposed to their blows, while the right could do nothing but remain spectators.

The attack was made on the 31st of May, and on the front of the Union troops; but, at the same time, a column moved on its flank, with the intention of taking possession of Bottom Bridge, and thereby forcing the four Union divisions into White Oak Swamp, where their destruction would have been certain. The front attack had raged for a long while, and the flanking column of the Rebels had nearly reached its destination, when it was attacked on its own flank by General Sumner's corps debouching over a bridge he had succeeded in throwing across the creek, which had not yet begun to rise. This attack creates disorder among the Rebels; their commander, General Johnston, in trying to retrieve the day, is severely wounded, and leaves the field. Night stopped the fighting, which, however, recommenced on the 1st of June, but without *ensemble* and *ordre* by the Rebels.

The attack, which had been a success at the commencement of the first day, ended with the retreat of the Confederates. Some 6000 to 8000 killed and wounded on either side, besides a few cannon captured by the Rebels, were the only result of this bloody battle. The remainder of the Union forces could not participate in the engagement, as at the moment the bridges over the Chickahominy were to be thrown, the creek rose, and even carried away part of General Sumner's bridge.

The time immediately following the battle was employed by both armies in intrenching themselves, and by the Union army, also, in building bridges, and thereby creating good communications between its right and left wings. In this way matters passed up to the 14th, when the uniformity of camp life was somewhat disturbed by the cavalry raid of Colonel Lee, at the head of 1500 men, in the rear of the Union army toward White House. This raid exposed at once the precarious and open position of the rear and the communications of the Federal army; and it would appear that the commander of the Union troops, in consequence thereof, took into consideration the change of base from the Pamunkey to the James River, which was open to his gunboats as far as Fort Darling; at least such may be inferred from orders, which he gave at that time, for transports with supplies to come up the James River.

While the armies were confronting each other near Richmond, the Confederate army at Corinth had retreated to Grenada unmolested by General Halleck. It was then generally and openly asserted that part of their force was coming East to join the army in front of their capital, and now commanded by General Lee, in consequence of General Johnston's wound. How far the reports respecting this reinforcement are correct, it is difficult to say; and though in the following battles the numbers of the Rebels were stated to be very great, the forces actually engaged do not by any means show such superiority.

In the north of Virginia, General Fremont found his position at Mount Jackson too exposed, and so he retreated. General McDowell, after his fruitless pursuit, takes position at Manassas Junction, and sends the division of General McCall, by way of Fortress Monroe, to the support of General McClellan. On the 26th of June, by an order of the War Department, the corps of Banks, McDowell, and Fremont were consolidated, and placed under the command of General Pope. In consequence of this order, General Fremont resigned, and the command of his corps is taken by General Sigel.

The excitement created in the army of the Potomac by Colonel Lee's daring raid had scarcely subsided, when another mysterious movement was observed at Mechanicsville Bridge. It was also ascertained that Jackson, with his force, was at Hanover C. H.

As in the following days, however, nothing of importance transpired, a forward movement was arranged for the 25th, and successfully executed. After a heavy skirmish, the Federal troops had advanced about a mile and held their ground. But the next day matters changed; the enemy, instead of attacking the Federal position in front, had crossed at Mechanicsville or Meadows Bridge, and were advancing against the right wing of the Union army, under General Fitz John Porter, consisting of two divisions and the reserve of regulars. General McCall being attacked, resisted successfully on the first day. In the night, General Porter's entire train was passed over the bridges on the right bank of the Chickahominy. General McCall retreated from his first position, and formed, with the divisions of General Morrill and General Sickles, a line of battle in front of Gaines's Mills. They were to pass the bridge on the evening of the 27th, and to execute with the army a grand movement through White Oak Swamp toward James River.

Early on the 27th the fight commenced, the Rebels pushing forward with the utmost determination ; the divisions of Slocum and Richardson are sent to the support of the right wing; the fight becomes so intense that all the reserves of the right wing are successively engaged; the enemy has the last reserve to give out, and he carries the day and victory with it. The left wing, formed by General McCall's troops, is entirely broken, and the disorder reaches even the center. Happily, night and two fresh brigades arrive—those of Meagher and French—which puts a stop to further pursuit.

In the night, the whole of the right wing passes the bridges over the Chickahominy; these bridges are destroyed, and the 28th finds the whole Federal force on the right of the creek. This same creek, which, on the 1st of June, had nearly caused the ruin of the army, proves this time to be its salvation. On the 27th an attack was also made on the left wing, to prevent this wing sending reinforcements to the right. This attack was, however, feebly executed, and without much result. The 28th and 29th were employed by the Federal army in passing its trains through White Oak Swamp, and by the Rebels in transferring part of their forces back to the right bank of the river. On the 29th, however, they attacked the rear guard of the army at Savage Station, but were repulsed. In the night, the Federal army retreated, and on the 30th it had passed through White Oak Swamp; and the advanced guard, conducted by Keyes and Porter, arrived the same day on James River.

A rear guard was left on the south side of White Oak Swamp, where several roads cross each other; under its protection, the trains arrively safely at Malvern Hill. This rear guard was, however, attacked with vigor by the Confederates; the Union troops fought with great bravery, and effected their retreat, repulsing nearly every attack. The last attack was tried against the whole Union force united on Malvern Hill, and covered by 300 pieces of artillery; the Rebels were obliged to retreat after having experienced heavy loss. From Malvern Hill, the army of the Potomac moved to Harrison's Landing, where its repose was little disturbed, except by occasional shelling from the other side of the James River, where the Rebels had concentrated part of their forces.

On the 11th of July, the Rebels had entirely disappeared from the front of the Union army. A reconnoissance, made by General Porter, found them, however, beyond Malvern Hill, and on their guard.

The army of the Potomac had been greatly diminished by the sword as well as by sickness, and the Rebel army had taken the offensive. It became evident that the total number of Union troops under arms was not sufficiently large to subdue the rebellion. A call for 300,000 more volunteers was made, and soon afterward another call for 300,000 militia men to be drafted for nine months. Stevens's division was recalled from Port Royal, and Burnside was withdrawn from North Carolina. These troops arrived in the course of July at Fortress Monroe.

At the commencement of August, some demonstrations or reconnoissances are made by the Union army in the direction of Petersburg. Finally, on the 12th of August, the army of the Potomac, not being strong enough to retake the offensive, commences its retreat by passing over the Chickahominy near its mouth. The march in the direction of

Yorktown, where it arrives on the 16th, is executed unmolested by the Rebels. At Yorktown, the army is re-embarked, and transported, partly to Aquia Creek and partly to Alexandria. General Burnside, with his corps, had sailed before, and had already occupied Fredericksburg. After its return, the army of the Potomac did not find much repose. It had scarcely arrived, when it encountered, in front of Washington, those same Rebel divisions it had left in front of Richmond.

General Pope, when he took command of the army in North Virginia, established his headquarters at Warrenton, where Banks and McDowell's corps were concentrated. General Sigel, with his corps, was at Sperryville and Luray, forming the right wing, and the troops at Fredericksburg formed the utmost left. General Hatch was ordered to advance with a brigade from Warrenton to Gordonsville; he went as far as Culpepper, pushing cavalry over the Rapidan to Orange C. H. From Fredericksburg a small cavalry force is also pushed southward to Beaver Dam, on the Richmond and Gordonsville Railroad. General Jackson is reported in force at Gordonsville, and consequently General Hatch retreated. On the 10th of August, General Jackson advances to Cedar Run, about six miles south of Culpepper C. H. Here he is encountered by General Banks; after a fight, in which General Banks's corps sustains heavy loss, and could only hold its ground when supported by fresh troops, General Jackson retreated, on the following day, over the Rapidan.

Soon after the battle of Cedar Mountain, General Pope is apprised that the Rebel army of Virginia is in motion against him. He commences, on the 20th of August, his retreat toward the Rappahannock to form a junction with General McClellan's troops, then beginning to arrive from the Peninsula. On the Rappahannock, the Rebels soon appear in front of him, making feints to cross the river above and below, while part of their forces in reality cross at Waterloo Bridge. General Pope being apprised of the fact, sends part of his force against the Rebels reported to have crossed. These Federal troops find a large Confederate force near Waterloo, which occupies them in front; while a large part of the enemy under General Jackson, having also a heavy force of cavalry with them, moves to Salem, and from there through Thoroughfare Gap to Manassas Junction. Their cavalry penetrates to Centreville and Falls Church; also up to the Potomac, in Loudon County, and to Winchester, in the Shenandoah valley.

At Manassas Junction, where the Rebel armies arrive on the 24th, they capture a large amount of government property. The force from Waterloo retreated toward Warrenton; and, on the 25th, when General Pope was apprised of the Rebel movement in his rear, he, on the suggestion of General Sigel, sent General McDowell and General Sigel to Gainesville, with orders to intercept communications between General Jackson and General Lee, the latter being still, with his main force, near Salem. General Reno, with one division, was sent to Greenwich to support, if necessary, General McDowell. General Hooker and General Fitz John Porter, who had already arrived from General McClellan's army, and who were stationed near Warrenton Junction, were ordered to march to Manassas Junction. One division was sent to occupy Thoroughfare Gap; finding it only feebly defended by the enemy, part of whose force were about to cross, the gap was carried, and, as the enemy soon afterward retreated, and no sign of his presence being left, this division quitted the gap to join in the fight in which the remainder of the Union troops were engaged.

General Hooker, on his march from Warrenton Junction toward Manassas Junction, encountered, on the 27th, the Rebel General Ewell, with his division, at Bristow Station, near Kettle Run, south of Manassas Junction. General Ewell is attacked and thrown back toward Manassas, whence he moves in the direction of Centreville. Another part of Jackson's force, on the 28th, in the morning, encounters General McDowell at Haymarket. This force is thrown back and unites with Ewell, who had fought Hooker the day before.

On the 29th, those Rebel troops take a position between Centreville and Haymarket, partly parallel to, and partly at right angles with, the Gainesville and Centreville Turnpike. In this position, they are attacked by the entire Union army under General Pope, but without definite result. The battle lasts till dark. In the night, the Rebels are strongly reinforced through Thoroughfare Gap by the remainder of General Lee's army. On the 30th, the fight recommences early in the morning, but does not take a decisive turn until the afternoon, when the left wing of the Federal army, under General Fitz John Porter and General McDowell, breaks, and the whole army is obliged to fall back beyond Bull Run.

During the same night, General Pope retreats to Centreville, where General Franklin, with his corps, had already arrived, General Sumner, with his corps, being still at Fairfax C. H. The loss in killed, wounded, and missing, as well as in artillery, was heavy. The next day, General Banks, who had marched from the Rappahannock to Brentsville, arrived in safety at Centreville.

The stay of General Pope at Centreville was not of long duration. On Monday, the 1st of September, the Rebels had turned his right flank once more, and pushed a column as far as Fairfax C. H. Generals Reno and Kearney were ordered to drive them thence; this was effected, but not without loss, the death of General Kearney himself being principally to be deplored.

The position at Centreville being too much exposed, General Pope commences his retreat, and seeks shelter under the guns of Washington. The same day, General Burnside was ordered to evacuate Fredericksburg, and to join the army of the Potomac with his corps.

Here ends this memorable campaign in Virginia, commenced by the Rebels on the defensive, and ended by a brilliant offensive, throwing the Union forces in disorder back to their first base of operation. But not only in Virginia had the Rebels taken the offensive. No; on the whole theater of war their armies proceeded offensively, attacking everywhere the Union forces, and invading the scarcely conquered States.

We left the Western armies after the evacuation of Corinth, the surrender of New Orleans, etc. On the 19th of July, General Halleck was called from the West to take the command-in-chief of all the United States forces. After his departure, General Grant occupied, with his army and that of General Pope, who was also called to the East, Jackson, Bolivar, Memphis, and Corinth. General Buell, with the army of the Ohio, moves back to South Tennessee and North Alabama. Nashville, Shelbyville, and Huntsville are occupied by his men. Cumberland Gap and Tazewell are held by General Morgan, with about 10,000 Federal troops. The Rebels have troops, under Generals Van Dorn and Price, near Holly Springs and Tupelo in Mississippi, which they had transported there from Arkansas; under Bragg, at Chattanooga, where he had arrived from Tupelo; and under Kirby Smith, in Eastern Kentucky and Tennessee.

In order to take the offensive, the different Rebel armies in Tennessee and Kentucky advance in several columns from the Cumberland Mountains, as a base of operation, against the communications of the Ohio army. On the 26th of August, they were reported, under Kirby Smith, in the neighborhood of Cumberland Gap, probably at Jacksborough. From there they marched into Kentucky. On the 29th, General Nelson is entirely routed by Kirby Smith near Richmond, Ky. Nelson falls back to Lexington, followed by the Rebels. From Lexington they push smaller bodies in the direction of Louisville and Covington, threatening thereby both those towns at the same time, and compelling the Union forces to divide for their defense; and in fact, great preparations are made in both places to repel an attack of the Confederate forces, which is hourly expected.

General Bragg, in his turn, is not idle. He moves to Sparta, Tennessee, thereby threatening to cut General Buell's communications with Nashville.

While those larger movements are being carried on, Western Virginia is scoured by Rebel cavalry and guerrillas, and the valley of the Kanawha is overrun by them. Some cavalry attacks are also made against Grant's army, to hold his force in check; and Washington, in North Carolina, is attacked by the Rebel forces.

General Buell, in order to counteract General Bragg's movement against his communications, concentrates his troops near Murfreesborough and McMinnsville, and marches them, about the 11th of September, to Nashville; but meanwhile General Bragg encounters this movement of the Union army by his advance into Kentucky, where he takes hold of General Buell's communications by his attack on Mumfordsville, at which place he obliged the Union forces, consisting of some 4000 infantry and several guns, to surrender on the 19th of September.

In West Tennessee, the cavalry engagements with Grant's army are followed by a more serious affair. General Rosecrans encountered General Price at Iuka, near Corinth, and, after a sharp engagement on the 20th, forced him to retreat to Tupelo; thence General Price marched to Ripley, where he forms a junction with General Van Dorn's forces.

In the utmost right zone the Rebels also operate offensively. Generals Rains and Hindman leave Arkansas, and march against Missouri.

General Buell, in order to prevent his being cut entirely from his base, marches to Louisville, leaving a strong garrison, under General Negley, in Nashville, which is fortified. The army of the Ohio begins to arrive, on the 24th of September, at Louisville, Bragg having, in the mean while, marched to Bardstown and Lawrenceburg. Humphrey Marshall, with about 5000 men, is at Paris, Ky., ready to join Kirby Smith. The different Rebel corps are approaching to form a junction at the decisive moment.

Meanwhile Nashville is invested by Rebel troops under General Breckinridge; they go so far as to demand the surrender of the city; which, however, is refused. The Rebel cavalry in Kentucky at the time performed many raids, and thereby created the belief that their force was larger than it really was. On the 28th, their cavalry entered Augusta, Ky., on the Ohio.

On the 17th of September, Cumberland Gap is evacuated by General Morgan, who retreats with his troops to Greenupsburg, on the Ohio, near Big Sandy River, where he arrives on the 4th of October, having been pursued all the time by Stevenson's and John Morgan's cavalry.

General Buell organizes and reinforces his army at Louisville, and retakes the offensive against the Rebels. On the 1st of October, a fight took place at Shelbyville, between troops from Louisville and those of General Buckner, whose main body was reported at Bardstown.

The different Rebel corps now begin their retreat, followed by General Buell. On the 8th of October, however, General McCook being too much advanced, and pressing the Rebels too closely, they make a stand, and defeat McCook at Perryville; but then resumed their retreat. At Harrodsburg, on the 10th, Bragg, Kirby Smith, and Humphrey Marshall united, and retreated to Camp Dick Robinson. On the 16th, Buell arrived at Crab Orchard, and the Rebels at London. On the 18th, John Morgan, with his cavalry, accomplishes a raid which has its parallel only in that executed by the Rebel General Stuart, between the 10th and 12th of the same month. He entered Lexington in the rear of Buell's army; marched to Versailles, Lawrenceburg, and Bardstown; captured several trains; made the entire circuit of the Union army, and left Kentucky, by way of Cumberland Ford, on the 29th of October.

In Western Tennessee, in the mean time, the Rebels had again taken the offensive, but were once more thrown on the defensive by General Rosecrans. On the 2d of October, a battle was fought between this general, with four divisions, and General Van Dorn's force, which we left at Ripley, and which had marched to Pocahontas, and thence to Corinth. The Rebels say their force consisted only of three divisions. After a desperate fight, lasting nearly three days, the Rebels were driven back toward Pocahontas, where they encountered General Ord coming from Bolivar. After another fight, and after having experienced great loss, they managed to escape across the Hatchie River, thence south to Holly Springs.

At the end of October, General Buell was relieved from his command, and replaced by General Rosecrans. But the Rebels under Bragg meanwhile have escaped through Cumberland Gap, and marched to Murfreesborough; and the army of the Ohio, giving up the pursuit, marched toward Nashville, where it began to arrive on the 8th of November. General Rosecrans himself reached this place on the 13th. Rebel cavalry occupied Somerset, in Kentucky. Price and Van Dorn meanwhile were fully employed in reorganizing their army at Holly Springs and Tupelo, where, on the 4th of November, General Grant commenced an offensive operation against them by marching toward Lagrange.

Before going further in the Western campaign, let us return to the East, where the offensive campaign of the Confederate army had not been of long duration, and had terminated in a similar way to that of the West.

After having forced General Pope to return under the guns of Washington, which retreat was executed in the greatest disorder, the Rebels marched in the direction of Leesburg, and, on the 5th of September, commenced crossing into Maryland. On the 7th, Frederick was occupied by them, and their cavalry pushed as far as Middlebrook and Poolesville. General McClellan meantime had taken command of the whole army—that of Pope as well as his own—and, on the 8th, commenced moving from Washington northward to meet General Lee. General Sumner this day occupied Darnestown. On the 9th, skirmishing takes place at Poolesville. On the 11th, Union troops occupy Sugar Loaf Mountain, near Monocacy Creek. The same day, the Rebels enter Hagerstown, and their columns have pressed from all sides toward Harper's Ferry. On the 12th, Frederick is entered by Union troops, who now push forward with great energy. On the 13th, the attack on Harper's Ferry had commenced. On the 14th, the Union troops, in their advance, encounter the Rebel rear guard at South Mountain and Crampton Gap; the former is occupied by General Longstreet, and the latter by General Jackson's troops. Reno and Hooker carry the first, Franklin the second—but too late.

This engagement, entered into by the Rebels merely to gain time for their operations against Harper's Ferry, has fulfilled its object. Harper's Ferry surrenders on the 15th. General White—who had occupied Winchester, and left it at the commencement of September, in consequence of the Rebels' advance, had marched to Martinsburg, but returned thence to Harper's Ferry to assist Colonel Miles—was included in the surrender, which delivered some 12,000 prisoners and great quantities of stores and ammunition into the hands of the victors. General Jackson, however, did not repose long on his laurels. Scarcely had the prisoners been paroled, when he resumed his march, and moved in the direction of Shepherdstown to join General Lee, who was posted near Sharpsburg, behind Antietam Creek, and was awaiting the Union army to give battle.

On the 16th, General McClellan's army arrived near the creek, and formed in line of battle opposite the Rebels. General Hooker, with his army corps, crossed the creek during the afternoon of the 16th, and had a preliminary engagement with the Rebels; and, on the 17th, the whole army advanced to the attack. Generals Hooker, Sumner, and Franklin, with their respective corps, successively attack the left wing of the Rebels, which, however, holds firm, though at first it loses some ground. Their right wing is assailed by General Burnside, who is thrown back to the bridge from which he debouched at first. Night closes in, and no decisive result has been gained on either side.

On the 18th, the two armies faced each other, without, however, engaging, both being worn out by marches and the previous day's fighting. The Union troops are reinforced this day, and during the night of the 18th the Rebels withdraw, in full order and great silence, over the Potomac. An attempt to follow them on the 20th, and to cross right in front of their army, fails, part of the troops, after having crossed, being repulsed with loss. After some demonstrations made in the direction of Williamsport, the Rebels retreat toward Winchester, taking position between this place and Bunker Hill. The Federal army does not molest them in this movement; but occupies Harper's Ferry, and encamps in Pleasant Valley, covering nearly the whole front from Williamsport to Harper's Ferry.

Nothing disturbed the repose of the two armies at the end of September or the commencement of October. Some reconnoissances were pushed toward Warrenton by General Sigel's corps; they found Rebel pickets there. Leesburg, Aldie, and Thoroughfare Gap were also occupied by them.

On the 10th of October, the repose of the army of the Potomac was somewhat disturbed by the news that the Rebels had entered Pennsylvania, and occupied Chambersburg. It turned out to be General Stuart on a cavalry raid. He had, with 1800 men, crossed the Potomac at Coy's Ferry, and moved to Chambersburg; this place he left to march toward Fredericktown; thence in the direction of the mouth of the Monocacy. Finding an infantry column there he turned to the left and recrossed three miles below, at White's Ford, carrying a great number of horses and other goods with him. The Federal cavalry arrived at the ford when the Rebels had passed; they had marched eighty-three miles in one march, just in time to see the last Rebel crossing.

After this remarkable feat, everything became quiet again; the only fact of importance being a reconnoissance toward Winchester, and the sending of some troops, under General Cox, into the Kanawha valley, in Western Virginia, to drive out the Rebels.

Finally, at the end of October, signs of a general advance became manifest; and in fact, the 1st of November saw the whole army of the Potomac moving down Loudon valley, leaving Harper's Ferry strongly occupied. The cavalry being continually in advance, had to fight its whole way against Rebel cavalry. On the 3d, the army reaches the Manassas Gap Railroad, most of the gaps in coming down the valley having been occupied.

On the 6th, Orleans and Warrenton are occupied; and, on the 8th, General McClellan is relieved of his command, and replaced by General Burnside. This change in the command occasioned, probably, a change in the plan of operation; and, at all events, some delay in the further advance. The army was camped near Waterloo, Warrenton, and the Rappahannock, guarding the fords from Waterloo to Rappahannock Station. Rebel cavalry was seen everywhere in front, flank, and rear of the Union army. Thoroughfare Gap was occupied by General Sigel.

On the 14th of November, the army left its respective camps and marched toward Fredericksburg. On the 17th, it arrived at Falmouth, opposite Fredericksburg, which was already found occupied by the Rebels. The army went into camp, forming a line of battle from Aquia Creek to Falmouth. The pontoon-train had not yet arrived, and therefore the passage could not be undertaken at once.

What the movements of the Rebels were during this time, is not very clear. It would, however, appear that part of their army marched at first in front of the Union army, retreating before it, and then moving parallel with it on the right bank of the Rappahannock; it arrived at Fredericksburg nearly at the same moment as the Union army; and that another part of their army remained quietly in the Shenandoah valley. This force appeared, on the 26th of November, near Salem, and then moved south and eastward, joining the remainder of the Rebel army, which was encamped, and extending itself on a range of hills, forming a semicircle around Fredericksburg; which circle having a radius of about $1\frac{1}{2}$ to 2 miles, was one of the strongest positions for a large army that can be imagined. At length the pontoon-trains arrived, and, on the 12th of December, the Federal army enforced the passage over the Rappahannock, throwing bridges opposite the town and three miles below. The passage was only feebly opposed, just enough to make a show of resistance.

The troops crossed, and, on the 13th, the main position of the Rebels was attacked; but after several useless attempts to carry the hills, the army, after a loss of from 10,000 to 12,000 men, was obliged to retreat, and seek shelter under its own guns. On the 13th, in the night, the army moved back over the river, which was accomplished without difficulty.

While this was going on in the north of Virginia, considerable activity existed at and near Suffolk, under orders of Major-Generals Dix and Peck, for a movement in the direction of Petersburg. After some fruitless demonstrations, all became quiet again in these parts, and the movement was not carried out.

In North Carolina, General Foster advanced from Newbern, with 15,000 men, to Kingston, which he took after little resistance; thence he marched to Goldsborough, where he destroyed the Wilmington and Petersburg Railroad, after which he returned to Newbern.

General Banks, after great preparations at New York, had sailed, on the 4th of December, for New Orleans, where he arrived on the 14th, part of his force being destined for an attack against Vicksburg and Port Hudson. He superseded General Butler in the command at New Orleans.

In Mississippi we left General Grant taking the offensive. He advanced with a large army, on the 3d of December, toward Holly Springs, the Rebels retreating southward, pursued by General Grant's whole force. General Hovey, with 20,000 men, moves from Helena toward Grenada to take the retreating Rebel column in flank or rear; but the Confederates change their course to the southeast and escape. On the 16th of December, after having moved ten miles south of Grenada, a further pursuit of the Rebel army is judged impossible. Hovey retreats to Helena, Sherman to Memphis, and Grant to Bolivar. The Rebels follow immediately, and defeat and capture, at Holly Springs, a small rear guard of several hundred men. On the 24th, General Sherman leaves Memphis with a large number of troops, and moves to Helena, from whence he embarks with his army to attack Vicksburg. Vicksburg meanwhile had been reinforced by troops from Arkansas, and Price and Van Dorn's columns were within supporting distance. When General Sherman therefore arrived, he found the place strongly occupied. He, nevertheless, attacked it on the 1st and 2d of January; but was repulsed with great loss. General Banks, from New Orleans, had not arrived, nor assisted with his troops and gun-boats in the attack.

In Tennessee we left the army of the Ohio arriving at Nashville, under the command of General Rosecrans. The Rebels meanwhile concentrated in the neighborhood of Murfreesborough, under the command of General Bragg. On the 6th of December, a Federal brigade is attacked in this place, and obliged to surrender. Finally, after all kinds of preparations and movements on both sides, General Rosecrans advanced, at the end of December, against Murfreesborough with about 50,000 men. An engagement ensued, lasting several days, in which the Federal troops at first experienced a severe check, but afterward recovered; and consequently, on the 3d of January, 1863, in the night, the Rebels retreated, though in good order, and unmolested by the Union troops, in the direction of Tullahoma.

Finally, in the utmost right zone, one more battle was fought, on the 8th of December, between the Rebel General Hindman and the Union Generals Blunt and Herron, near Prairie Grove, Arkansas, in which the Rebels are defeated, and obliged to retreat into the interior of the State.

Here ends the narrative of the campaign of 1862. It is more than probable that some mistakes will have occurred; and, considering the present state of affairs, it is scarcely possible that it should be otherwise. I have not access to any official documents, except those published by the public press. The whole campaign I had to put together by searching the files of several newspapers. It is well known how many false reports are published; how incorrect dates are; how rumors are given as facts; and how incomplete most of the statements are for the purposes of a work like mine. There is, in most cases, no notice of the starting of a body of troops, or of any movement, till fighting turns up somewhere, and then one has to find out where the troops came from, etc. Of the movements of the Rebel armies scarcely anything is published except rumors, and their numbers are always so variably stated that hardly any reliance can be placed on the statements about them.

I hope, therefore, that the reader will excuse the mistakes, and the apparent want of connection in the above sketch; the more so, as it is only the text of my disquisition. As the discussion of these facts is simply an abstract and scientific one, the same lesson may be derived from a wrongly-stated case as from a rightly-stated one, provided only that the facts be rightly discussed.

The review of this campaign—a campaign so full of vicissitudes—is, perhaps, one of the most profitable studies in which an officer can engage, as nearly all the successes, and, without exception, all the great failures of both parties may be assigned to the direct violation of the great rules of military science. In order to render the review, which we are about to undertake, clear, we will commence with the plan of the campaign, embracing the whole theater of war, and then proceed to the discussion of the operations as they took place in the three zones separately.

Let us refer to Map III: we find there the position of the different Union armies at the time they were ready to start. Curtis and Pope in Missouri; Grant and Buell in Kentucky, besides some small forces in East Kentucky and Western Virginia; Banks at Winchester; the army of the Potomac at Washington; a large force at Fortress Monroe; Burnside at Roanoke; Hunter at Port Royal; and Butler's expedition getting ready for New Orleans. Thus, there were not less than ten different armies, and as many different lines of operation, acting all in a more or less concentric direction toward the interior of the theater of war. Not one of these armies was so strong that the Rebels might not with ease have concentrated a stronger one against it.

If we consider what has been said in Chapter I. in reference to great invasions, it will be remarked that this plan of invading by a great number of lines of operation, having a concentric direction, has never been followed by the great captains, either of ancient or of modern times; and in fact is entirely against the rules laid down in Chapter I. It is a division of force, and it is acting on exterior lines.

The campaign, or rather the plan of the campaign, had some resemblance to the invasion of France in 1793. The result was partly like that of this invasion, and would have been still more so, had the Rebels taken a lesson from Carnot, and followed from the first his plan of defense.

As we have seen in Chapter I., a plan of invasion like this is based on simultaneous action on many points; the defense, on the contrary, is based on successive action against one point after another. To make such a plan really successful, a simultaneous energetic advance of all the Union forces should have taken place; and then, perhaps, full success would have been obtained, not because the plan was good, but because the defense at first committed the same mistakes as the attack, and even more. But the impossibility of such simultaneous action was soon made manifest.

The importance of the various points being different, the defense had made very different preparations in the three zones; and thus it happened that, while some of the invading armies had conquered large tracts of country, others had scarcely moved from their base of operation. Consequently, the unity of action was entirely broken. Scarcely had the first operation taken place, when nearly all connection between the several lines of attack in the three zones ceased, and each commander, on a separate line of operation, acted according to his own judgment. There was no unity in effort and purpose, and consequently no decisive result.

We have said that the defense committed the same mistake as the attack did. The number of fortified positions, and the small bodies of troops, clearly showed the intention to defend a front of operation of nearly 1500 miles on all points. These long lines of defense, though they cover everything, may be pierced wherever we choose to attack them; and when broken on one point, the whole line is obliged to fall back. The correct defense would have been to concentrate a sufficient force south of Nashville; to oppose Grant, Buell, Pope, and Curtis only by small corps of observation, retreating to the main body, which should fall on Grant or Buell—according as which of the two should present himself first—defeat him, and then the next one, and so on. And even if we take a still more extended view of the question; if we consider that the Confederate government depends entirely on its army, and exists only so long as this is successful, we may truly say that the real seat of government of the Confederate States, their real capital, is at the headquarters of their army, and not in any particular town or place. If we take this view of the question, and apply the principles of defense to the present case, all the Union armies, including that of the Potomac, should only have been opposed by small bodies of observation, and the main army of the Rebels should have been in a position between Knoxville and Lynchburg—that is, in the center of the entire theater of war—whence they might have fallen like an Alpine avalanche on any Union army invading their territory. Finally, it will be observed that, in the general plan of the campaign, as it is before us, the distribution of troops was not in accordance with the importance of the three zones. In fact, deducting the men in hospital, and those still in the recruiting districts, probably the real number of men fit for duty at the opening of the campaign did not exceed 450,000. Of these nearly 100,000 were in Missouri, and only about 150,000 men, forming a field army, were in the left or decisive zone. A large proportion of them was used up in the occupation of fortifications and important points. The superiority in the right and center zones was great; consequently operations in these zones advanced more quickly than in the left zone.

An inspection of the map, as well as what has been said in Chapter II., will show us that a Union army holding Kentucky and Tennessee could be taken in flank by a Confederate army moving from Lynchburg and debouching through Cumberland Gap, and that this Union army could be thrown back from South Tennessee to the Ohio by such an offensive movement. By this we mean that, should Kentucky and Tennessee have been carried by Union troops, but the Federal army in Virginia have experienced a decisive disaster, one single march of the Rebels from the springs of Big Sandy River toward Mumfordsville, Louisville, and Cincinnati would compel the Federal forces to evacuate the conquered country. That this is true, the march of Bragg and Kirby Smith has shown. Buell was thrown back by this march from Huntsville and Florence, in Alabama, upon Louisville, in Kentucky, a distance of not less than 300 miles.

In her wars with France, where Italy was the disputed apple, Austria always thought that the chief object was the occupation, in force, of the country. She had to learn more than once, to her cost, that Italy was more frequently conquered in the valleys of the Rhine or the Danube than on the banks of the Mincio or the Po.

In like manner, Kentucky and Tennessee will be conquered on the banks of the Potomac or James River, rather than on those of the Cumberland and Tennessee Rivers, and, until decisive results are gained near the James River, advantages in the West will be more or less ephemeral.

To conclude, therefore, the discussion of the general plan, we shall merely say that we miss in it the full understanding of the great principles of wars of invasion. The invading army should not care for towns or for occupation; it should have but one object—the finding and annihilating of the enemy's armies. We also miss the full understanding of the theater of war and its great strategic features. In a word, instead of one grand war or grand plan of operation, half a dozen small wars or petty plans were substituted. Let it be remarked here, that the defense admirably profited by the rude lesson it had received at Fort Donelson, and that from this moment its action became more and more correct, and in accordance with the rules: to concentrate the main force always on the decisive point, and to act on interior lines.

**Operations in the Right Zone.** — The plan of campaign for this zone, framed separately, so far as may be guessed from the operations, seems to have been very simple. General Curtis had to clear Western Missouri of the Rebels and to penetrate into Arkansas, and General Pope had to move along the Mississippi and to open this river to the Federal gun-boats, which, by ascending the rivers of Arkansas, would divide this State into several parts, cut the communications between the different Rebel corps, and facilitate the operations of General Curtis, by furnishing supplies and protection. There is nothing to be said against this plan, as General Pope's as well as General Curtis's army were both sufficiently large to fight single-handed any force the Rebels could bring against them in those parts.

The operations in this zone are so few, and, compared to the whole, so unimportant, that it is scarcely worth while to mention them. There are, however, two or three movements which deserve to be noticed. Price, we have seen, retreated before a superior Federal force under General Curtis; but immediately on entering Arkansas, the Rebels proceeded to a concentration of their forces, and from the defensive they passed to the offensive. General Van Dorn executed a movement which reflects credit on him. With his whole force he turned the Union army, seizing its communications, and forcing it to fight when cut off from its base of operation. The battles of Marengo, Ulm, Jena, and Auerstadt were fought under similar circumstances. Only one objection—and it is an important one—is to be made, viz., that it was not safe to execute this movement against an army superior in men and armament. Van Dorn was beaten; and the only thing which is astonishing is, that our army did not make better use of the advantage it had when on the line of the communications of the defeated army.

The next movement worthy of remark is General Curtis's advance into Arkansas, after the battle of Pea Ridge, and his retreat to Helena, on the Mississippi. This movement, though a retreat, but to an accidental base of operation, had the character of an advance. General Curtis, once in Arkansas, gave up his base of operation on the Upper Mississippi, and his lines of operation connecting him with it, to take up a base on the Lower Mississippi, by way of an accidental line of operation.

**Operations in the Center Zone.**—The operations in this zone are important and highly instructive. The Ohio, being the only line separating this zone from Union territory, becomes evidently the base of operation for the Union army or armies acting in it. Not less than three or four armies invade it simultaneously: General Pope, with his army, on the utmost right, along the Mississippi; General Grant, along the Tennessee River; General Buell, along the Louisville and Nashville Railroad; and finally, some smaller corps in the direction of Cumberland Gap.

The plan of operation in this zone, to judge from the movements the army and navy actually performed, was to conquer Kentucky and Tennessee, and to open the Mississippi to Northern navigation, thereby separating the right zone completely from the center zone; and having the Mississippi with its affluents under full control, operations could be directed in the right or center zone with equal facility. The Union forces being in possession of the line of the Tennessee, the States of Mississippi, Alabama, and Georgia found themselves pretty much in the condition treated under the base of operation, Fig. 1, Chapter I.

Had the entire theater of war been composed only of the center and right zones, this plan would have had great merit. It is in fact based on a division of the enemy, and of a division which is complete. The party holding the Mississippi could throw the superiority of forces into one, and then into the other zone, without fear of the enemy being reinforced, and his armies would then be successively crushed.

But the right and center zones were not the entire theater of war; and this changes the question so completely, that the plan which would have been a correct one under the first supposition, becomes entirely incorrect according to the real state of affairs. It is easy to show this.

Let us first suppose that the two zones we are speaking of form the whole theater of war, and that the Savannah, the Clinch River, the Upper Tennessee, (as far as Chattanooga,) and the Big Sandy River are boundaries toward a neutral State. Considered as such, the natural line of invasion would evidently be the Cumberland or the Tennessee, which would play here the same part that the River Meuse plays in Belgium, in a strategical point of view. Smithfield or Paducah would be the base of operation. Following the course of these two rivers, a Union army would take hold at once of the communications of a Rebel army stationed, for instance, near Louisville. This Rebel army would have to retreat, by way of Nashville or Sparta, with the utmost speed, or it would be obliged to fight a battle in which it would have to face south. Should defeat be the consequence, it would be thrown in the direction of the Ohio, with a certainty of destruction. We said it could only retreat by way of Nashville or Sparta; and in fact it could not cross the Big Sandy River nor the Cumberland Mountains, as these, according to our supposition, are boundaries of a neutral country. In like manner, as the line of the Tennessee River takes in reverse the whole of Kentucky and Tennessee east of it, so it does with the country west of it, and situated between itself and the Mississippi—that is, if the passage over the Mississippi is interrupted for the Rebel army. The consequence is, that if Clinch River were the boundary of a neutral country, the march from Paducah to Florence, in Alabama, would carry the entire upper center zone, and the simple occupation of Florence with a large army would be sufficient to maintain it. Thus, with the aid of the gun-boat flotilla, expeditions might be made to open the whole course of the Mississippi, leaving it to the vigilance of those gun-boats to render the separation between the right and center zones effective. A greatly superior force might now be thrown into the lower center zone, so that the adoption of two lines of operation would be justified. Acting, then, similar to what we have already described in Chapter III., when speaking of the invasion of this part of the theater of war, the conquest of this zone would offer no difficulty; there would be only the difference, that the Savannah is replaced by the Mississippi, and that, instead of making the invasion from east to west, it would be made from west to east. The Rebels, continually outflanked by the army coming from the Tennessee, and pressed in front by that coming from the Mississippi, would be obliged to leave Mississippi, then Alabama, and would finally be thrown into the east corner of Georgia or into Florida.

This whole plan of operation is, however, changed by the simple fact that the Clinch River is not the boundary of a neutral country, but of the left zone, or the most vital part of the entire theater of war. What before in our supposition was impossible—the retreating of a Rebel army to and over Clinch River—is now possible, and it will therefore be seen that a Union army, marching along the Cumberland from Smithland to Nashville, does in no way cut a Rebel army in Kentucky from its communications, and in general does in no way clear Kentucky of the Rebels, as they have always their retreat open along Big Sandy River or to Cumberland Gap; therefore, the Cumberland or the Tennessee line, which was decisive according to our supposition, is no more so in reality, though it is an advantageous line.

Be it now remarked that, whatever the military operations in the center zone may be, Louisville and Cincinnati are of sufficient importance to require an army for their protection and that of the country round them. If this army is destined for active service, the most natural line of operation—at least the easiest one, and that offering the greatest facility for communications with the base—is evidently the line from Louisville to Nashville and Huntsville. Should this line be adopted in consequence of the facilities it offers, then another army and line of operation become necessary to act against Cumberland Gap or the mountain district in general.

Therefore if, under the circumstances as they were when the war broke out, the upper center zone is to be conquered and occupied and the Mississippi to be opened, we are almost necessarily led to the adoption of four lines of operation: One along the Mississippi, to open the river to navigation; one along the Tennessee and Cumberland, to open these rivers and to outflank the position which the enemy may hold along the Mississippi or the Louisville and Nashville Railroad; one along this railroad; and one from Louisville, in the direction of Cumberland Gap. To have four lines of operation in so restricted a space is against all rules of military science; and as the plan of operation we have deduced from the movements of the Union army, as they actually took place, is scarcely to be executed otherwise—certainly not with less than three lines—we conclude that the plan is not sound, or not adapted to the circumstances and the strategical features of the theater of war.

There is in the execution of this plan another fact which is worth mentioning, and which strongly militates against its adoption. It is evident that the conquest and occupation of the upper center zone is only a preliminary measure for the conquest of the lower one. It is the first object to be attained. Considering, then, the four lines of operation with respect to the second object, the conquest of the lower center zone, it will be remarked that the Louisville and Huntsville Railroad is the most direct line from north to south, besides being the principal line of communication. This line would, therefore, be chosen in preference to any other for a southward movement, and also for the occupation of Kentucky, and of Tennessee itself. But this line is nearly parallel with the Cumberland Mountains in its whole length; and as the Rebels may choose the Tennessee or these mountains (as they please) for a base to start from for action in Kentucky and Tennessee, the Cumberland Mountains will offer them the advantage of being able to act against the communications of a Union army in North Alabama, at any moment they choose to do so. This is a truth which has been proved by Bragg's invasion of Kentucky; and if another proof is wanted, it may be found in the resemblance between the relative position of the base of operation of the defense to the line of operation of an invading army in Kentucky and that of the French in the Peninsular war. In that war the line of operation of the French armies extended from Bayonne to Burgos, Madrid, Cordova, and Seville. The base of operation of the English army was Portugal; first Lisbon alone, but after the capture of Badajos and Ciudad Rodrigo by Wellington it was pushed to the frontier. The line from Ciudad Rodrigo to Badajos is parallel, or nearly so, to the line from Burgos to Seville.

In all their offensive movements, the English acted directly against this line of communication of the French. In 1808, Moore, in his offensive movement, marched from Ciudad Rodrigo toward Valladolid, Napoleon being with his whole army at Madrid, an army nearly twice as large as that of Moore; besides, Napoleon was not the man to permit playing with his communications. He immediately threw himself on Moore's communications, and the disastrous retreat of the latter to Corunna was the consequence. In 1809, Wellington also moved against this line of communication, but the battle of Talavera having crippled him too much, he was obliged to retreat; the more so, as Ney and Soult were marching against his own line of operation.

Finally, in 1812, after having defeated Marmont in the battle of Salamanca, Wellington advanced straight against Burgos from Ciudad Rodrigo as a base, and this was decisive. Soult, who held Seville, was thrown back to Madrid, and Andalusia was conquered and cleared from French occupation on the banks of the Douro.

This relative position of the base of operation for a Rebel army and the line of operation of the invading Union army, necessitates a strong occupation of the country, as it facilitates all kinds of raids and expeditions against the railroad communications of the Union army.

Occupation is division of force, and the more occupation is necessitated, the more chances an enemy will have to beat the occupying army in detail. The rout of General Nelson at Richmond, Ky.; the surrender of from 4000 to 5000 men at Mumfordsville, on the Louisville and Nashville Railroad; the capture of a brigade at Murfreesborough by

John Morgan, are but too palpable proofs of the truth of our reasoning.

Not only do Kentucky and Tennessee require a large number of troops for occupation, but the Mississippi requires a still larger. This river once opened, all places where main lines of communication arrive near it, connecting the right with the center zone, must be guarded by large detachments; the consequence of which will be, that the active or field army in these parts will be seriously reduced; and should the enemy, by conducting his defense correctly, destroy this field army, the loss of all the detachments would probably ensue.

For these reasons we conclude that the main plan of operation was not based on sound principles and a thorough understanding of the country; that it was in its execution complicated; and that it necessarily led to operations which were not correct. The defense at first made a still greater mistake. It is, in the very nature of things, that a country adopting the defensive is the weaker one, and under such circumstances the right application of the maxims of war becomes an imperative necessity. Here, on the contrary, the defense opposes every advancing Union army by a smaller but intrenched Rebel army. The long line of defense is easily broken at Fort Donelson, and all the trouble of fortifying Columbus, etc. goes for nothing; besides, there cannot be any doubt that the Rebels did not understand at first the advantage they might derive from the strategical features of the country. Finally, the greatest blunder they committed was the omitting to take advantage of the errors or of the bad plan of operations of the Union army. Fort Donelson, however, taught them a lesson, and they profited afterward by it.

From the general plan, let us pass to the details of the operations as they took place in this zone.

We have just said that Fort Donelson was a lesson to the Rebels; in fact, immediately or very soon after its capture they evacuated their other strongholds, and commenced concentrating at Corinth. Grant, meanwhile, had pushed south as far as Savannah, Tenn., Buell was in Nashville, Pope still at New Madrid. General Grant, with about 50,000 men, passed the Tennessee at Pittsburg Landing, and encamped his army at Shiloh, backed by the river. This is a favorable opportunity to destroy a Union army, and immediately the Rebel commanders take the necessary steps for a concentration of troops to profit by the occasion. Bragg from Mobile, Polk from Columbus, Johnston from Murfreesborough, join Beauregard, who is already at Corinth. Grant is attacked and defeated; and had there been a little more of that iron energy which usually distinguishes great commanders, the Union army would probably have been destroyed, notwithstanding the presence of the gun-boats and the arrival of Buell. Buell, informed perhaps of the great concentration of the Rebel forces, hastened, in turn, to a junction with Grant. He arrived in time, not to retrieve the day on the 6th, but to win another battle on the 7th. The Rebels were beaten on the second day by the application of the very same principle which made them gain the first day's battle. What would have happened had they been 15,000 men stronger, that is to say, had the disaster of Fort Donelson not occurred in consequence of their defective defense?

What would have happened had their plan of operation from the very first been based on a similar concentration, so that Grant might have been attacked several weeks sooner? We do not wish to indulge in speculations, but it is easy to see how much more the chances would have been in their favor. The consequences of the first mistake were felt throughout the whole campaign. The plan of the battle and the conception of the whole manœuvre is creditable to the Rebel generals who executed it. The concentration of troops, and, still more, the immediate resumption of the offensive after a disastrous battle, is highly creditable to the officers and men of the Union army. The Rebels were, however, not followed up after the second day's battle; and this was a great mistake—just as great a one as the Rebels committed in not pushing the battle on the 6th, and following it up to the very utmost.

There are two kinds of battles in which the pursuit should be very differently conducted. The first is, that in which the battle is the consequence of a strategical manœuvre, by which we have gained the communications of the enemy. In such a battle, all that is generally needed is simply to repulse the enemy, and to operate or pursue him so that he cannot escape either to the right or left. His whole army will then finally be obliged to surrender. The second is, that in which we encounter the enemy, both parties having their lines of retreat free. In this case the pursuit must do the principal work. Rear guards must be crippled, and every effort made to break up the main army. To abandon the pursuit is to give up the fruit gained by the victory.

Here, in our case, the fault was aggravated by the whole

position of affairs. Supposing that Buell and Grant were too crippled after the battle to follow immediately, they might have been reinforced within six days by General Pope, who had New Madrid and Island No. 10 in his possession. Then, from Shiloh to Corinth being only twenty to thirty miles, the army might have been before Corinth ten days after the battle of Shiloh.

There is no doubt that after this battle the Rebels were quite as crippled as the Union army. This latter, being reinforced by Pope, would have had, therefore, a decided superiority; and that, even later, it possessed this superiority after the Rebels had had time to be reinforced, is easily perceived from the fact that had they been so sooner than the Federal army was by Pope's arrival, they would have moved once more to Shiloh, and refought the battle of the 6th.

Eight to ten days after the battle of Shiloh, the fortifications of Corinth were probably not very strong; and if they were, a simple march or movement to Waterloo, Alabama, and thence to Jacinto and Danville, Mississippi, would possibly have induced the Rebels at once to leave Corinth; and then, by marching direct to Ripley and Holly Springs, the Union army might probably have prevented the Rebels from retreating south, and have forced them to a disastrous and decisive fight.

Instead of such rapid action and decisive direction of the line of operation and of pursuit, the Union army advances slowly against Corinth, which the enemy meanwhile strongly fortifies. The Federal troops besiege Corinth till the Rebels, probably sorry to give them so much trouble, evacuate on the 30th of May. They retreat to Grenada; and, as if the occupation of Corinth was the main object, the Union army remains there! General Pope alone undertakes the pursuit, as if he by himself could accomplish, against a not defeated army, what he, united with Buell and Grant, could not do!

The Rebels posted at Corinth were caught *en flagrant délit.* A Union army was between them and their Eastern armies; and by acting with the left, the Union army might have brought about a decisive, and, to the enemy, a disastrous battle. Neglecting to take advantage of an enemy's faults is decidedly blundering, and here the fault was irreparable; for these very Rebel troops were afterward transported East, and performed their share in inflicting the disasters which befell the Union armies there. The consequences of one mistake are sometimes incalculable in war, as well as in life in general. It is with them often as it is with an Alpine avalanche—growing, growing, till they crush everything under their enormous weight.

After the occupation of Corinth, the main object of the Western campaign seemed to have been attained. General Grant commenced the occupation of the country west of the Tennessee, by placing his troops near Memphis, Corinth, Bolivar, and Jackson, in Tennessee, and Columbus, in Kentucky. General Buell left, on the 10th of June, for South Tennessee and North Alabama, moving from Corinth in the direction of Chattanooga, a distance of two hundred miles, or ten to fifteen days' march. That it was the intention of General Buell to go to Chattanooga, is difficult to say, as he might have been there by the 25th of June. We only know that in July he was still in the neighborhood of Huntsville.

In the Rebel army, General Bragg had superseded General Beauregard. After their retreat to Grenada or Tupelo, the Rebels soon corrected their mistake of forming exterior lines with their Eastern armies, by moving as quickly as possible from Tupelo to Chattanooga, this Badajos of the upper center zone. In fact, the position of Chattanooga, in respect to Northern Alabama, is nearly the same as that of Badajos in respect to Andalusia; the former being invaded by a Union, the latter by a French army.

Buell's line of retreat from Huntsville to Nashville was within the grasp of the Rebels concentrating or arriving at Chattanooga; and the first use they made of their new combination was the surprise and capture of the Union troops which were stationed at Murfreesborough, probably to guard the communications of the Ohio army. This army, finding its line of communication and retreat endangered, had only the choice between two alternatives. Either to advance to Chattanooga with all its force, or to retreat and take a position near Shelbyville or McMinnsville—that is, nearer to its temporary base, which was Nashville.

Whether Chattanooga was takable or not at that time, I do not know. To attack it was certainly a risk, considering that the Ohio army would have had to move through a mountainous country easily defended, and to go so much farther from its base. However, all depended on the strength of this army. The very least that Bragg could concentrate would probably have been something like 35,000 to 40,000 men; and certainly only a greatly superior force should have tried to dislodge them from the strong positions in the interior of these mountain regions, unless a previous defeat in the open plain had taken place.

If, therefore, the strength of the Ohio army did not surpass 30,000 to 40,000 men in the field, or available for operations, it would have been folly to march to Chattanooga; and the only thing to be done was to concentrate near Shelbyville or McMinnsville, and to offer battle there. This latter expedient was the one General Buell chose. The Rebels, however, declined fighting; but, by moving still to their right, they turned once more the position of General Buell, and thereby forced him to retreat to Nashville, where he arrived on the 11th of September.

The whole configuration of the southern part of Tennessee is such that it is difficult for an army in the plain to take the offensive, especially if not sufficiently strong; but the army holding the mountains has it entirely in its power to pass from the defensive to the offensive. The inactivity of the Ohio army is thus explained; not so that of the Rebel army, which took nearly two and a half months to do what it might have accomplished in three weeks.

By the force of circumstances, and the strategical formation of the country, the Ohio army was put on the defensive, and followed, therefore, the impulse of the attack. The attack was slow at first in the execution of its movements, and the defense, occupying the enemy's country, was evidently in no hurry to give this up.

We must remember another thing here. The different commanders of the Union forces were independent of each other; every one acted in his own department as he liked, and cared very little as to what his neighbor was doing. This was only the natural consequence of having half a dozen lines of operation.

Troops had been left in Eastern Kentucky to hold Cumberland Gap; to defend Lexington, Louisville, Cincinnati, etc. The Ohio army was as little affected by the fact that General Rosecrans had been attacked at Corinth, as by the fact that General Morgan or Nelson had been, or could be, attacked elsewhere. These generals had to look out for themselves, just as the Ohio army had to look after its own safety. Very speedy action on the part of the Ohio army against Kirby Smith, in Eastern Kentucky, could therefore not be expected up to the moment that this Rebel general's action would endanger its safety.

We conclude, therefore, that (the circumstances being such as we have stated) the action of the Ohio army was correct, or at least not incorrect, in its movement from Huntsville to Nashville. We say if the circumstances were such as we have stated; because we found the greatest difficulty in tracing the lines and the movements of the contending armies in these parts from the newspaper reports. A great number of details and facts which might materially change the aspect of affairs, and especially the criticism thereon, are probably unknown to us.

There was, however, one decided mistake made in this campaign; it was, that the Ohio army was not ordered to march, or did not march, from Corinth to Chattanooga, by forced marches, as soon as the Rebels had retreated from the first of these two places, and the pursuit had been given up. It might have been there by the 10th or 15th of June, which was probably sooner than General Bragg's arrival there. After the arrival of this general with his force, it was too late.

Scarcely had General Buell commenced his retreat, when the Rebels immediately pushed forward with their right. A corps was left at Sparta, and the remainder moved to Mumfordsville, forcing from 4000 to 5000 Union troops to surrender. The troops left at Sparta moved parallel with General Buell as soon as he left Nashville.

Considering the position of the Ohio army at Nashville, we shall find that it had only the choice between two lines of conduct. Its real base of operation (Louisville) was endangered, and its communications already seized. It had therefore to do something to prevent being cut off entirely, or of being left without supplies. The first expedient was to retreat to Louisville with the main force, leaving Nashville fortified, and in the hands of an able commander, with a small corps; the second was, to throw itself, with the entire force, on the communications of the Rebel armies, by marching to Carthage, Tennessee, and thence to Burkesville and Somerset, Kentucky.

A similar course was proposed by Soult to King Joseph, after the battle of Salamanca. Wellington was near Burgos, and the king ordered Soult to evacuate Andalusia, and to join him south of Madrid. Soult, unwilling to give up Andalusia, proposed to the king to unite his (the king's) force and those of Suchet with his own troops, and to move from Seville to Ciudad Rodrigo—that is to say, on Wellington's line of operation. The king refused, in consequence of the general state of affairs. The campaign against Russia was a failure, and the French armies could not be exposed to risk.

The circumstances were somewhat similar here. The peninsular campaign against Richmond, as well as that of Pope in Virginia, had been failures. The Rebels were in Maryland. For General Buell to throw himself on the communications of the enemy, would have been equivalent to giving up entirely his own. To be defeated in such a position would have been ruin, and the battle would have had a decisive influence on the whole war. Therefore, the most prudent course was evidently to march to Louisville, leaving a sufficient garrison in Nashville. The very moment General Buell thought it a risk to fight a battle with the Rebels on his communications, it would have been a mistake to fight along his march; because, up to the time when he really arrived at Louisville, he was continually so placed that the Rebels might have thrown him back upon Nashville, or into the Ohio.

Both cases would have been equally disastrous. Therefore, taking into consideration the general state of affairs, no reproach can be cast on the Ohio army for its retreat to Louisville, so far as principle is concerned. Had opportunity occurred for beating the enemy in detail, and been permitted to slip away, this would evidently have been a mistake, and a most serious one too.

We have not been able to find any indication of the time the different marches and movements took, and are therefore entirely unable to discuss this part of the question, though it is an important one.

Once arrived in Louisville, the Ohio army was largely reinforced. It advanced against the Rebel armies, which then united and retreated to Cumberland Gap. The pursuit was carried only as far as London, Ky., probably in consequence of the difficulty of maintaining the troops. The Ohio army went back to Nashville, and the Rebel army returned to Chattanooga, thence to Murfreesborough. The operations of the different Rebel armies all round rendered the position at Cumberland Gap a precarious one, and it was consequently evacuated by General Morgan. Should the fact be correct that he had to fight his way to Greenupsburg, and that he lost no cannon nor part of his train, then no doubt this retreat would be creditable to him and his men, and very little to the generals who permitted him to escape.

The plan of the invasion of Kentucky, as conceived and executed by the Rebels, deserves great attention. Let us, before entering on the consideration of it, say only, that if Chattanooga holds a similar position to that of Badajos, Cumberland Gap, in its turn, plays the part of Ciudad Rodrigo. Kirby Smith marched from Cumberland Gap, or the neighborhood, direct to Lexington, and Bragg advanced from Chattanooga against General Buell's communications. The Rebels form two lines of operation in this movement, but they were very careful to maintain interior lines; besides, Kirby Smith had no enemy of importance before him, and his object was only to threaten. Under these circumstances two lines may be adopted. In this invasion the Rebels made the best use of the direction of their base of operations, relative to the line of operations of the Union army. The consequence was, that by one march they cleared nearly the whole of Tennessee and Kentucky of the

Union troops, and threw Buell from North Alabama back on to the Ohio. So long as they had no strong enemy before them, they divided to attack, to occupy, and to threaten many points at the same time. As soon as a Union army in force approaches, they unite their divisions to avoid being beaten in detail. In their offensive movements, they capture or beat all smaller detachments stationed round for the occupation of the country. In their retreat, as soon as they are pressed, they make an offensive return at Perryville, defeat the Union advance guard, and continue their retreat unmolested; Bragg, in this retreat, changes his natural line of retreat to Chattanooga to an accidental one, that of Lexington to Cumberland Gap. Therefore, the direction of action and the action itself were correct in this invasion, and the plan, as well as the execution of it, so far reflect credit on the general or generals who originated and carried it out. There is only one remark to be made, and it is an important one. The invasion of a country must have an object, and the object should be important enough to compensate for the risk the army runs in making it. Here, in this invasion, the Rebels declined fighting a decisive battle; their sole object was, therefore, merely the destruction of the small detachments of Union troops and the provisioning of their own army; for they could not expect to hold Kentucky and Tennessee without destroying at least the main army that occupied it. Had they destroyed this main army, to commence with, then they would have been able to hold the two States. In fact, it was the Ohio army which formed the nucleus of the army which drove them out of Eastern Kentucky; had it been destroyed at the very first, it could not have been reinforced by Grant's divisions nor by innumerable old and new troops which joined it at Louisville. Therefore, to render the invasion decisive, they ought to have commenced with a sufficiently successful blow, and not with a raid; and, considering the position of the different armies, we believe that a first success could have been gained.

The army of the Ohio, when near Huntsville, probably did not muster more than from 30,000 to 40,000 men. Bragg had perhaps some 25,000 to 30,000; Kirby Smith, including Humphrey Marshall's and other small detachments, 15,000 to 20,000; finally, Price and Van Dorn, who had come from Arkansas, are said to have had at that time 38,000, which number, however, we believe to have been exaggerated. Kirby Smith was at Cumberland Gap, about 150 miles distant; Price and Van Dorn at Tupelo, about 200 miles, or 10 days' march, distant. Could these different corps have been united without General Buell's becoming aware of it, the Rebel army, about 60,000 to 70,000 strong, might, in two forced marches, have moved to Manchester and Shelbyville, taking hold of General Buell's communications, and forcing him to fight facing northward; if defeated, (which would have been probable against such odds,) he would have been thrown into the Tennessee by a vigorous pursuit. Here the first success would have been obtained, and then, dividing in order to beat the smaller detachments, threaten different points, invade, in fact, the whole country, would not only have been correct, but of more lasting effect. The only difficulty is to make a concentration without the enemy becoming aware of it. For this purpose several things are required; and we may learn much from Napoleon's conduct. First, the march of the different corps, coming from different sides, must be so timed and calculated that they shall all arrive on the same day, and the day afterward the offensive movement must commence. Secondly, all movements—the preliminary march for the concentration as well as the offensive movement itself—should be executed by forced marches of from 20 to 25 miles a day. Thirdly, the troops should be kept in ignorance of their destination; the rumor of a different destination to the real one should be spread among them. Finally, the principal generals of the joining corps, at least those of well-known name—such, for instance, as Kirby Smith or Price—should not leave with their troops, but stay with a detachment of several thousand, with which to make demonstrations and great noise in a very different direction from that in which their main body has moved, so as to show themselves in very distant regions, and then, a few days before the arrival of their columns at the place of rendezvous, they should start, and, by traveling 100 miles or so a day, arrive at the same time as their men. By managing matters in this way, and telling no generals, except the commanders of corps, of the plan, a great concentration might be effected without the enemy becoming aware of it until at the last moment, or when it is too late to remedy.

Napoleon, when about to start for the invasion of Belgium against Blücher and Wellington, gave the most brilliant feasts. In the night, in the middle of one of these feasts, he disappeared, and started for the army by extra post. This was so well managed that he was for two days with his army, and all his troops were in movement, before Wellington could believe the fact, being informed by good authority that Napoleon was still in Paris. Part of the English army was consequently surprised in its quarters, and its junction would perhaps have become impossible, had it not been for the double mistake of the 6th army corps, which assisted neither Ney in the battle of Quartre Bras nor Napoleon in that of Ligny.

Only after a concentration of his forces with those of Price and Kirby Smith, would General Bragg have been justified, we think, in attacking General Buell. With his force alone, a battle would probably only have been detrimental to his cause, or a useless butchery, as he could not have expected to gain any decisive result with an army inferior in strength to that of his enemy; but had such a concentration and action by the Rebels taken place, the final result of the Western campaign would have been probably very different from what it really was.

The next movement we have to consider is the battle of Corinth. Price and Van Dorn unite to attack General Grant's army, and to beat him in detail. Their first march from Ripley to Pocahontas is very correct; they take thereby a central position between Bolivar and Corinth, and prevent the junction of the Union troops stationed at these places. In the further execution of their plan, they however made a mistake. In movements of this kind, the general rule is first to beat the corps or army which has its line of retreat open, while the corps which is cut from its communications by the manœuvre is amused by a small corps, just sufficient to force it to display. By attacking

Corinth in the rear, as they did, without first beating the troops at Bolivar, or even without masking them, they exposed themselves to an attack in their rear by all the troops at Bolivar, while they themselves were engaged in front with those of Corinth, as in fact it happened. What the reasons of their defeat at Corinth were, after they had carried the fortifications, it is difficult to say; one thing is certain, viz., that the defense of the place reflects great credit on the Union general and men. Once beaten, the Rebels retreated to Pocahontas; but here they encountered General Ord, who had been sent to attack them in the rear; they opposed this general, however, and thereby gained time to pass the Hatchie River. When the last Rebels had disappeared, General Ord's column found itself face to face with a column of Federal troops coming from Corinth; the Rebels had just slipped off between the two columns. It would seem that, had General Rosecrans marched at the same time with his whole force to Black's store, and thence to Nubbin's store, the Rebels might perhaps have been entirely captured or destroyed. The position after the battle was such, that only a small corps should have pursued in the rear, but the main body should have pursued on the flank. Being more to the south than the Rebels, it might have continually prevented the Rebels retreating southward. They could only have escaped by opening their way with the bayonet. This attempt might have been somewhat difficult, considering that they had already been beaten, and that Ord's column was coming close at their heels.

Finally, there is one more operation in this zone which

deserves notice. It is the advance movement of the Mississippi army, under General Grant, to Grenada. With this direct movement, a flank movement by General Hovey, with 20,000 men, was executed from Helena toward Grenada. I do not know how many thousand men Price and Van Dorn had under their orders, probably more than 20,000. Hovey arrived first at Grenada, and, therefore, the Rebels might have beaten him before General Grant's army reached that place; at all events, Grenada was within their reach, and they could have prevented the junction. Hence this operation was wrong in principle; it was the adoption of two lines of operation, acting in the attack in a concentric way, one of the acting armies being weaker than the enemy, who holds a central position, and the point of junction being within his reach. The Rebels made a blunder in not taking advantage of the fault committed by the Union commanders.

**Operations in the Left Zone.**—This zone is the most important of the three. Hence the operations in it were the most important; and as in some respects they offer novel features, they are highly interesting and instructive.

The question practically solved in the campaign which we are going to pass in review is this: Is a country, having a large army of several hundred thousand men, but also a very large navy, and being at war with its neighbor, with which it has a common boundary of several hundred miles, to be considered as a naval or as a continental power?—that is, ought it to carry on the war according to the principles which an insular power like Great Britain would have to follow, when making war on a continental power, or would it have to follow the principles of great wars of invasion, as carried out by great continental powers when invading their neighbors?

To render the understanding of the proposition easy, suppose France and Germany engaged in a war. The common boundary extends over some 400 to 500 miles. The French frontier is covered by a great number of fortresses. France possesses a very large navy, and great means of conveyance; Germany does not. France and Germany each possesses armies of over 700,000 men strong. The question at issue now is, would France, by invading Germany, be justified in giving up the advantage of a frontier of 400 miles, to form a line of operation such as England would, based on the sea and on its ships? Would she be justified by taking, for instance, Stettin as a base, covered by a large fleet, and starting from that point an army against Berlin, instead of starting it from the Rhine, and at the same time that offensive operations are going on in the east, leaving an army based on its fortresses on the Rhine on the defensive?

This was the experiment which was tried in the operations of the left zone. I believe the experiment might have been dispensed with, for the following reasons:—

1. To act on one point offensively, and on the other defensively, is evidently forming two lines of operation, or dividing the army into two parts. Admitting the principle to be a sound one, that whenever two lines of operation are required, it is always better to act offensively, first on one point, and then on the other, by transporting the mass of troops from one to the other, and leaving the weaker always on the defensive; admitting, I say, this principle to be

sound when two lines are required, the only questions to solve are, are two lines of operation really required, one being always preferable? and if so, have they exterior or interior lines of communication?

It is obvious that a country having several hundred miles of boundary in common with its neighbor, and its frontier well covered with fortifications, so as to form a good base of operation, has no need of forming two lines of operation —one by land and one by sea. Besides, the very nature of two such lines of operation renders them exterior in respect to those held by the defending army. The consequence is, that the defending army, by making use of the long frontiers, throws its whole mass into the interior of its enemy's country, and beats him in detail, while his main army is engaged on the coast disembarking material, troops, etc.

2. In great operations, speed and punctuality are two main requirements. Therefore the more an operation, or the machinery of an army, etc. can be simplified, the more can be done with it. By making a combined operation —that is to say, one in which the army and navy are engaged—great difficulties immediately arise, and speed, and still more, punctuality, become impossibilities. First, the navy is under a different command, and then its supplies depend on different quartermasters and commissaries. In its operations, the weather plays a great part. Another difficulty is to find transports for a large number of troops. It is not only the men, but the horses, wagons, cannon, provisions, stores; all must be sent by these transports. The expenses are enormous; the time lost is generally very great; the means of transport usually

insufficient; unavoidable sources of delay are continually arising; disorder is, in most cases, the natural accompaniment of these operations; and speed and punctuality are at an end. For forming an idea of the immense means of transport required for large armies, and the whole way in which such movements should be prepared, the study of Napoleon's preparations in 1805 will prove a good school.

Most of these combined operations therefore infringe upon the principal rules of military science, especially when they are executed against a bordering country. They are based on a division of force; they involve the formation of two or more lines of operation, with exterior lines, against an enemy holding a central position; there is no certainty in results, no punctuality, and no speed; and there are enormous costs, without adequate returns for the outlay; they are therefore to be avoided when possible.

The principal plan of the campaign in the left zone was composed of one of these combined operations. In fact, as far as we can judge from the operations, and from what has been published on the subject, the general plan was to fortify Washington strongly; to have it well garrisoned; to hold Harper's Ferry and the line of the Potomac by smaller corps; and to transport the main army, by means of the navy, to a point as near as possible to Richmond, the capital of the Confederate States.

The point chosen for the debarkation was Fortress Monroe; and the main direction for the line of operation was the James River. It was probably thought that on this line gun-boats might penetrate the river, and powerfully assist in the capture of Richmond; besides, York and James Rivers, if once in the possession of the Federal navies, were excellent lines for supplying the army.

Before entering upon the discussion of this plan of operation, let us say a few words about its object, which was obviously the capture of Richmond.

The reasons for which wars are undertaken are manifold; and according to the real nature of the war, the object to be attained greatly varies. If we wish only to recapture a province taken from us in a previous war, we may be satisfied with occupying the province, and maintaining it against the enemy's armies. In this case we do not care so much to destroy the enemy, which always requires a great effort, and is joined with risk to ourselves. We are satisfied to hold him off, and push him back from the ground we have won. We capture the fortified towns, and, after a time, the enemy, seeing his efforts unavailable, and being afraid of losing more, makes peace. Such, for instance, was the Crimean war. A great war of invasion was out of the question; and all that was desired was the capture of the Crimea, perhaps not even that. Russia, after the reduction of Sebastopol, probably afraid that the whole of the Crimea might be captured, made peace. In such cases, the first and main object of a campaign is the capture of a place, a fortress, or a tract of land; but in no way the conquest of a whole country, combined with the destruction of all its parts capable of resistance.

Very different from wars of this kind are those which have a greater object—the conquest of a whole country, for instance. Conquest is only complete when all resistance has ceased. The first or the main object of the campaign (not of the war) is therefore the utter destruction of all the armed forces of the enemy, wherever they may be found. This accomplished, the next or second object is the occupation of provinces and towns, and the capture of fortresses. How little, for instance, the occupation of provinces, towns, and even capitals interferes with real *military powers*, is proved by history in many wars.

In the Seven Years' war, the Russians captured Berlin, but were obliged to relinquish it, and the war was in nowise finished by the capture. After the battle of Salamanca, Wellington committed the extravagancy of entering Madrid in triumph, instead of falling on the different isolated French corps. The consequence was, that he had to leave it in his turn, and to retreat to Portugal. In 1805 and 1809, the occupation of Vienna by Napoleon would not have finished the war, had it not been for his after victories at Austerlitz and Wagram. Finally, in 1812, the occupation of Moscow, in the very heart of the Russian empire, did not lead to peace, and did not prevent, but on the contrary hastened, the invading army's final destruction.

Richmond, the Confederate capital, is to be considered as the seat of a real military power, whose very existence is based solely on the success of its arms. Such a government has a residence, but not a capital. In fact, no old traditions make Richmond a place of importance. What matters it if Richmond be in danger of being captured? The leaders of the rebellion go twenty or forty miles farther off, and all is said. Their orders will not the less be executed, nor will their armies fight the worse for it. In fact, they ought never to have given any place even the appearance of a capital.

It is very different with Washington. Washington is the history of the Union; it is the seat of the loyal government, fighting for the suppression of the rebellion, and is supposed to be doing so supported by the majority of the whole country. Let Washington be taken, and the loyal government be overthrown, the consequence would be, that rebellion would become the legal authority, as it would have the appearance of having the majority on its side; and the North would have to acknowledge the independence of the South, or to submit to be governed by it.

The difference in the relative importance of Washington and Richmond is therefore great. The capture of Washington by the Rebels might finish the war; but the capture of Richmond would probably not have more influence on the ultimate result than the capture of Nashville, Memphis, or New Orleans.

We conclude, therefore, from what we have just said about the first object of a campaign in a war of conquest, that in the plan of operation, such as was executed in the left zone, a secondary object—the capture of Richmond—was made a main object; and that consequently, whatever the plan for the attainment of this object may have been, no decisive result could have been gained by it, the object remaining the same.

Let us now pass in review the plan of operation before described.

The general principle of it is treated above when speaking of combined operations, and in our case we will easily see that two lines of operation were formed when a single one might have been chosen with facility; that, moreover, these two lines had exterior lines of communication, and that a central position was held by the enemy; and finally, that as far as speed and punctuality were concerned, scarcely anything worse could have been imagined. From Washington to Richmond by land the distance is about 125 to 130 miles, or 6 to 7 days' march. From Fortress Monroe to Richmond it is 75 miles, or 4 days' march. The army had advanced to Fairfax C. H. and Centreville, about 20 miles from Washington; thence they had to return to Alexandria to get re-embarked, making some 30 to forty miles marching before embarking, or 2 days' march, which, joined to the 4 from Fortress Monroe, makes 6 days' march, or about the entire time required to march from Washington to Richmond. The fact is, that in order to avoid 15 or 20 miles of marching, 100,000 men, with their immense material, were transported 180 miles by water, and to avoid this 1 day's march, not less than 19 days were spent in embarking, transporting, and disembarking the army. Speed and punctuality were evidently here entirely out of question.

Having considered the plan of attack in general, that is, the correctness of forming several lines of operation by a combined operation of army and navy, we have now to consider the direction of those two lines.

One line had for its base Washington, with its fortifications; its natural direction was the straight line from the Federal capital to the Confederate one. On this line the defensive was chosen. The other line, the offensive one, was that from Fortress Monroe to Richmond—that is to say, from the sea-coast into the interior of the country. In Chapters I., II., and III. we have at some length proved that operations made along the sea-coast, or generally to the left of the main left zone, are far from being decisive, for the very simple reason that the Rebel army can always retreat, and continually maintain its interior lines of communication with the Western armies, by which it can be reinforced, and finally repulse the invading army. Besides, the Union army, once really thrown against one of the large rivers or bays, might, if rightly attacked, even find the protection of the gun-boats unavailable, and be obliged to surrender—that is to say, the Union army voluntarily places itself in positions into which the Rebel army ought to be forced by grand manœuvres. Hence the operation is in no way decisive for the Rebels, but might become so for the Federal army, the very reverse of what ought to be.

Two lines of operation imply that two objects are to be attained. The object of the offensive operation is evidently the main object; it is, in fact, the object of the campaign. On the contrary, that of the defensive operation, or of the operation of the defensive army, is secondary to this principal object, the main force being evidently employed for the offensive operation, as the whole campaign is to be an offensive one. At the time this campaign was planned, the Rebels were supposed to have very nearly as large an army as that of the Union, and their position, continually threatening Washington, was certainly far from being defensive. How would it have been if the Rebels, basing themselves on the difference of importance between Richmond and Washington, had adopted for defense a plan of campaign similar to that of the attack? To be more clear—if the Rebels had opposed the Potomac army coming from Fortress Monroe by a small corps, just sufficient to retard its march, and force it to a continual display of force, and had in the mean time thrown themselves by forced marches with their main force on the smaller corps in front of Washington; if then they had passed the Potomac, captured Harper's Ferry and Baltimore, and attacked Washington on the left side of the Potomac, giving up, meanwhile, Richmond, and acting upon the simple truth, they could always afford to lose Richmond if they capture Washington instead. This they might have done, and hence we conclude that the choice of the direction of the two lines of operation, as well as their importance, was not well considered at the time this campaign was planned. The principles laid down by the Archduke Charles, that in war we should always act as if the enemy would do the very worst he could do to us, was certainly not taken into account. Recapitulating, therefore, all that has been said of this general plan, we may come to the following conclusions:—

1. All main operations conducted to the left of the main left zone, that is to say, along the sea-coast, will force the Union armies to the adoption of two lines of operation, one defensive and one offensive; or, in other words, to a division of force, to protect Washington and to carry on offensive operations, as the Rebels, by choosing a position on the right flank of the Union army, threaten, without any danger to themselves, Washington and the Union army.

2. All operations to the right of the main left zone do not require this division of force. The garrison of Wash-

ington might be reduced to a few thousand men, as the Rebel army could not act against Washington with the Union army on its left flank, giving it thereby free access to its line of retreat and its interior lines of communication with the Western armies. If it did, nevertheless, act against Washington under such circumstances, the Union commanders could only congratulate themselves, as this action would insure the destruction of the Rebel army by attacking its left flank and throwing it into the Potomac.

3. The strategical direction of a line of operation in the left portion of the main left zone can never be decisive; while, on the contrary, the strategical direction of a line of operation along the right of the main left zone is decisive.

4. Combined operations of army and navy, being out of the control of the Commander-in-Chief, are to be avoided, as no speed nor punctuality can be accomplished by them; besides, as above shown, the strategical direction of the line of operation not being decisive, no adequate result is obtained for the immense cost of such expeditions.

5. From 1, 2, 3, and 4 we conclude that *one* line of operation to the right of the main left zone would be correct and preferable to the formation of more lines, which we know to be incorrect, or which at least is in general to be avoided.

Let us now pass to the actual details of the campaign.

The first movement is the expedition of General Burnside to Roanoke Island. As to its general fitness, the following remarks will apply to all smaller similar expeditions. They are to be considered as detachments sent to the rear of a stronger enemy, and consequently they are against the rules of grand war. Whenever the enemy chooses to do so, he may crush them; besides, they conduct only to a division instead of to a concentration of force; and the alleged reason, that they are necessary to prevent foreign intervention or the running of the blockade, is simply ridiculous, for this reason, that were the operations conducted rightly, with the great superiority of men possessed by the North, the war ought not to last longer than two or three months, as shown in Chapter III.; and in these two or three months certainly foreign powers would not have much time to meddle, nor would many ships be able to run the blockade. For more on the subject of expeditions, see "Summary of the Art of War," pp. 52 and 168.

As far as the execution of the operations against Roanoke Island is concerned, nothing is to be said except that it seems to have been carried out well and even brilliantly.

The operations of the army of the Potomac began with General Banks's movement against Winchester. Scarcely had the Union army advanced in this direction—that is to say, on the right of the main left zone—than the Rebels evacuated Centreville. If this evacuation was the consequence of the above movement, and I really do believe that it was, it would show that the Rebels understand fully the importance of the different parts of the theater of war, though at that time their other preparations for the defense of their country were far from being good or correct. Two days after the retreat of the Rebels, the whole Union army moved after them, but only as far as Fairfax and Centreville, for no other purpose than to move back again, to embark at Alexandria.

The embarking of the Potomac army commenced on the 17th of March, and lasted until the 5th of April. It took not less than nineteen days to transport 80,000 to 100,000 men a distance of 180 miles, in which nineteen days the army might have marched some 350 miles, or very nearly from the Potomac to the Savannah. The troops were landed near Fortress Monroe. By consulting the map, it will be seen that Fortress Monroe is situated at the end of a peninsula, which in some places is not over six to seven miles wide, and in all about fifty miles long. A line of battle six to seven miles long requires, according to the nature of the ground, and to its being defensive or offensive, from 40,000 to 100,000 men. (See "Summary of the Art of War," p. 76.)

The ground on the peninsula being extremely favorable to the defense, 40,000 men could at any time have stopped 100,000 men for a long while, if the army would have had to make the whole march from Fortress Monroe to the upper end of the peninsula—that is, if, by means of the gun-boats and steamers, the York and the James Rivers could not have been ascended, and thereby the Rebel army outflanked.

The James River, at the time the operation took place, was closed by the Merrimac, and the York River by Yorktown and Gloucester. The army therefore had to advance from Fortress Monroe; and as the peninsula is so narrow that no flanking movement could be made, all movements had to be executed by the front, and every obstacle to be carried by force.

One of the chief principles of grand war is to get possession of the enemy's communications without exposing one's own. Evidently the application of this principle was out of the question in the position the Potomac army was placed in. To suppose that by transporting the troops to Fortress Monroe, and by acting thence against Richmond, was seizing the communications of the Rebel army in Virginia—at Centreville, for instance—is to suppose that the Rebels could neither see, nor think, nor march.

They were, at the time the first preparation was made, in possession of the right bank of the Potomac, and could see and count the transports going up to Alexandria. Even if transportation for half of the army had been provided, it would have taken five to six days to transport the whole of it; and in six days the Rebels could have marched from Centreville to Williamsburg, and encountered the Union army in front again. These considerations alone should have been sufficient to prevent the campaign on the peninsula.

While the Potomac army found itself imprisoned on the small tract of land between the intrenchments of Yorktown and Fortress Monroe, the army for the defense of Washington was divided into three independent commands: Fremont, in the mountains west of the Shenandoah; Banks, in the Shenandoah valley; and McDowell, east of the Blue Ridge. Thus, including General Burnside's corps, not less than five armies were operating on five different lines of operation against Richmond. A curious spectacle—the main army shut up in the peninsula, and these other four small armies inviting the enemy to come and annihilate them! The Rebels, however, were magnanimous! they allowed this unique opportunity of striking a decisive blow (we might almost say, to finish the war) to slip. What an occasion for a general ambitious of gaining the reputation of a great commander! Jackson finally felt that cheap laurels might be gained here, and he made the attempt, though commanding but a small corps. He could not help gaining some laurels, though not enough to enable him to pass for a great captain.

These surrounding manœuvres, forming four or five lines of operation converging all on one point, were favorite manœuvres in the good old times. In the Peninsular war, the Spanish generals used them profusely. In the first war of the French revolution, the Austrian generals could not live without them. In more modern times, however, they had become scarce; till in our present day, the Virginia campaign saw them once more in full flower.

It is scarcely worth while to say much about such dispositions; history has already pronounced judgment on them. To form an idea as to how much they are against the rules, and how ridiculous they must be considered, if executed against a stronger army in a central position, it is only necessary to read military history; to study Jomini, Napoleon, Cesar, and all those who have won a name in the great art of war.

After the evacuation of Yorktown, the army followed up the Rebels, whose rear guard was found at Williamsburg. Meanwhile General Franklin's division was transported to West Point to act on the communications of the Rebels. At Williamsburg, the Rebels made a stand, and were only forced to relinquish the position in consequence of a flank movement executed by General Hancock. The whole movement, as well as the style in which it was executed, is highly creditable to this general.

After the retreat of the Rebels, the army remained for several days at Williamsburg, which delay must be considered a fault. We must look at such a pursuit as was executed by Napoleon, after his great battles of Jena and Wagram, or at the pursuit executed by Blücher, after the battle of Waterloo, to see what, under such circumstances, can be and should be done.

Here was a rear guard of the enemy which ought to have been crippled before arriving at the Chickahominy, and not even trying to cripple it was certainly a fault. Admitting that the roads were bad, they were quite as bad for the retreating as for the pursuing troops. Besides, Franklin's expedition to West Point could be of no avail, if not supported immediately by the whole army coming from Williamsburg. As a general rule, detachments like that of Franklin seldom do any good in the rear of a stronger enemy, and, when against great captains, nearly always finish with disasters.

The defense was well conducted. The evacuation of Yorktown, just as that of Centreville and of Corinth, was executed in a masterly manner. The leaving of a rear guard at Williamsburg was also right, and according to the rules, in order to prevent the enemy following with too much impetuosity, and to give the trains time to be brought in safely. For similar reasons, the engaging of Franklin was in its place.

The army took eleven days to move from Williamsburg to White House, a distance which it ought to have made in two or three days at the very utmost. These delays, and this great slowness in a forward march, are fatal mistakes. They give an enemy time to make his preparation; to recover from a fatiguing retreat; to push in reinforcements; to get over the demoralization which the retreat may have occasioned among the troops; to restore discipline, etc.; and instead of a half-beaten enemy, we find a strong and determined one in front of us.

These slow movements violate the greatest rules of grand war, which are to use the utmost speed, and always to strike an enemy before he is prepared. The movements of Cesar and Napoleon, and some of the French marshals in the Peninsular war, are well worth studying in respect to the use of time.

When the army arrived on the Chickahominy, it placed one wing on the right and the other on the left bank of the creek, connected with each other only by way of Bottom Bridge. Very soon after its arrival, an attempt was made to form a junction with General McDowell at Fredericksburg. This attempt was based on sound principle, and would, in some degree, have corrected the defective position of the Union armies; though it is by no means proved that had this junction taken place, it would have insured the capture of Richmond. The Rebels could have prevented it by moving in force on Hanover C. H.; by beating Porter and McDowell, and throwing them back to the north, and then placing themselves between these two generals and General McClellan's army.

The disposition of the army in separate wings was a very dangerous one, as is well proved by the two attempts the

Rebels made to destroy these wings separately. The first of these two attempts was made against the left wing, and the battle of Fair Oaks was the consequence of it. The left wing consisted of four divisions in echelons, one behind the other along the York River Railroad. The Rebels fell on these divisions in front, and at the same time moved a strong column against Bottom Bridge to cut off all retreat, and prevent any reinforcement arriving.

The conception of this plan was certainly sound. The idea was not to defeat, but to destroy the left wing—that is, nearly one-half of the Union forces. To attack with their concentrated force part only of the Union army before they could be succored, is according to the rules of war. The conception of the plan, and the applying of the rules to the situation, reflect honor on the general who was the author of it. The execution of the plan, however, was far from being equal to the conception. This is probably, to a certain extent, the consequence of the composition and organization of the armies, which possess too few well-instructed officers, and men not sufficiently drilled, to permit of very rapid or very precise manœuvres.

The promptitude with which General Sumner marched against the enemy in this battle is creditable to him; and here the old truth was once more verified, that he who flanks, exposes his own flank. The flanking column of the Rebels was attacked on its own flank by General Sumner; the disorder created thereby, occasioned in a great measure their final repulse. The plan of defense in this battle was not equal to the plan of attack.

With the exception of General Sumner's corps, the right

wing did not succor the left wing; and though there were difficulties to overcome, they ought to have been overcome at all events, and at any price. When the battle commenced, some uncertainty was entertained about the real place of attack. It might have been that the fight on the left wing was only a feint, and that a main attack on the right wing would take place. All doubts were, however, soon dispelled. The reports from the battle-field, and an æronautic reconnoissance, soon proved that the whole Rebel army before Richmond was engaging the left wing. As soon as this fact was ascertained, three kinds of measures ought to have been taken at once. First, the immediate construction of bridges over the Chickahominy; the immediate marching of Sumner's troops to Bottom Bridge, and thence to the battle-field; and the immediate concentration of the troops more to the right, near the bridge constructed by the engineers of General Sumner's corps. The right wing would have had only some eight miles to march by acting so; and by commencing the movement at two o'clock, the whole army would have been by night on the other side. Troops, on such occasions, cross the defile in double quick, and the artillery is only brought on after the main body of the troops has passed.

That such or a similar energetic action was required, a simple reasoning proves. Three alternatives were possible. Either the left wing gains a victory; or it is only able to repulse the attack, and the result is a drawn game; or it is defeated, and may be entirely destroyed. The first of these three alternatives was out of question. It could not be supposed that four divisions would gain a decisive victory over the whole Rebel army. By not succoring the left wing, therefore, only a drawn battle or a disaster could be expected. By throwing five or six divisions to the support of the four already engaged, a drawn battle would evidently have been changed into a decisive victory, and a disaster probably into a drawn battle. The only objection which can be made to this reasoning is that, by throwing the whole army over the Chickahominy, the whole army was exposed to destruction. Admitting the cogency of this argument, we can only ask, how it happened that under such circumstances the left wing was placed on the right bank of the creek at all? and why Sumner was sent over? which, according to the supposition, would only have increased the disasters; and finally, why, if such a disaster was apprehended, the immediate retreat of the left wing was not ordered? Therefore, it was decidedly a mistake that the right wing did not succor the left wing; and that no bridges were ready, cannot be accepted as an excuse, considering that General Sumner managed to have one, and that, therefore, the other corps might have had bridges too. The crossing of the right wing ought to have taken place, even if no immediate advantage in the battle of the 31st of May could have been expected from it; it ought to have taken place, in order that the army might have taken the offensive itself immediately after the repulse of the Rebels. We can here only repeat what we have already said, of not following up a victory, when speaking of the battle of Williamsburg. That immediate action after a battle, even in this country, and with our present armies, is possible, is proved by the Rebels in the seven days' fight and by their campaigns in Virginia and in Maryland, and by the energetic advance of the Union army after the fight at South Mountain.

Jackson's offensive operation in the Shenandoah valley was one of the most apropos movements executed during the war; it prevented the junction between General McDowell's and General McClellan's troops; it threw the whole army in and around Washington on the defensive, and thereby prevented reinforcements being sent to the army of the Potomac, which was left to its own fate, and had finally to succumb under the blows its stronger adversary was about to deal it. The strategical direction of Jackson's line of operations was a good one. General Banks's corps was not only the weakest, but it was the center of the long line of defense or attack formed by the three Northern armies. By breaking this center, by beating Banks, General Jackson found himself at once in a central position, between the corps of Fremont, McDowell, and Banks, and the only mistake the Rebels made was to undertake this operation with about 15,000 men instead of 40,000 to 50,000.

It has been stated that General Jackson had 25,000 men. I do not credit this statement. With 25,000 men there was no reason to run away before General Fremont or before General McDowell, who came presenting themselves to his blows from two different sides, with only 15,000 to 20,000 men each. If Jackson had really been as strong as was stated, he ought, after driving General Banks over the Potomac, to have marched to the encounter of Fremont, beaten him, and then, turning against McDowell, driven him right under the guns of Washington. That with 25,000 men such action would have been possible, is sufficiently proved by Napoleon's campaign of 1796. Therefore, admitting that General Jackson had 25,000 men, is admitting that a blunder was committed in sending Fremont and McDowell on converging lines of operation against him; it was exposing them uselessly to be defeated separately, as in fact happened to them at Cross Keys and Port Republic, though Jackson had, all told, probably not more than 15,000; which may also partly be inferred from the fact that in these two engagements he had only 5000 opposed to Fremont and 8000 opposed to Tyler, making a total of 13,000.

In his advance, General Jackson did not march straight against Strasburg, but to Front Royal, whence he could act, and in fact did act, on General Banks's communications. But from Front Royal he did not choose the best line he might have chosen; he moved to Middletown, which is from Strasburg only half the distance from Front Royal; therefore Banks could sooner be there than Jackson. There are two other roads—one to Newtown and one to Winchester—from Front Royal, and the distance on these two roads is the same as from Strasburg to Newtown or Winchester. Starting, therefore, at the same time as General Banks, Jackson, by moving on one of these two roads, might have prevented the former from going farther north, and have forced him to fight a battle, the result of which would scarcely have been doubtful. A few cavalry thrown out toward Middletown, to disturb or even seriously attack General Banks's train, would probably have retarded this latter sufficiently to give Jackson time to be first on one of the two decisive points named above. On reading over the details of this operation, it seems, however, as though either General Jackson's force had not entirely arrived at Front Royal when the capture of the Union forces took place there, or else precious time was lost by him at this place, and the Union forces at Strasburg thereby enabled to make good their retreat.

The quickness with which General Banks understood the position and decided to retreat is creditable to him; but, as no further danger for his communications existed the moment he had reached Winchester, the retreat from this place farther north might have been conducted with more firmness and in a more soldier-like manner. What may be done under such circumstances, is well illustrated by General Sigel's retreat previous to the battle of Pea Ridge. In his case the superiority of the enemy was far greater than that of Jackson over General Banks, who had probably never to deal with more than 5000 to 6000 Rebels—that is to say, with the advance of their columns—his own command consisting of two brigades.

General Jackson's retreat from Winchester to Stannardsville was, as far as we can judge, executed in a masterly manner. His two engagements at Cross Keys and Port Republic show firmness and understanding of the art of war. The action at Cross Keys is highly creditable to the Rebel general and to his men who fought it. The general, on the contrary, who lets slip the opportunity of crushing 5000 men with 20,000, and, what is worse, who permitted himself to be beaten under such circumstances, has certainly but very few claims to the title of "general."

The direction chosen by the corps of Fremont and Mc-

Dowell, for the intercepting of Jackson, was a wrong one. To march to the place where Jackson had only been heard of, according to the last accounts, was evidently coming too late. To effect the object, a very simple exercise of arithmetic would have shown where to march to. From Winchester, where Jackson was on the 25th, to Harrisonsburg, in the Shenandoah valley, is three days' march; from Franklin, where Fremont was, two; and from Falmouth, where McDowell's corps camped, three forced or four ordinary days' march. Both Union generals might have gained certainly one, and McDowell easily two days' march on Jackson, who could not have been immediately informed of their movements. Hence, if General McDowell had marched to Stannardsville, and thence through Swift Run Gap to Luray, occupying Chester Gap and the road to New Market, Jackson could not have hindered him from doing so; if at the same time he had pushed a column from Warrenton to Manassas Gap, which could easily have been occupied and held by a small force, he might have been in those places on the fourth day, and formed by his left wing a junction with General Fremont, marching from Franklin to Harrisonsburg, and moving thence upon Broadway and New Market. Both generals, pushing rapidly forward and throwing out cavalry to the right and the left near the gaps, to remain well informed of Jackson's movements, might have been in this position on the fourth day; and, supposing they had gained only one day on Jackson, he could not have prevented them. It will be seen that, by acting in this way, they might with their main force have continually prevented Jackson returning south, whatever course he might take, as they could always reach the decisive point before him. That point would have been evidently the spot to the right or left, where Jackson tried to pass them. That they would have gained several marches on him, is well proved by the fact that at the commencement of June he was still at Strasburg, and on the 7th only at Port Republic, at which place, or somewhat below, the two Union generals might have been by the 29th of May.

While Jackson was retreating, leaving the armies of the North out of breath with their useless run, the army of the Potomac remained inactive, permitting the enemy to recover from his repulse at Fair Oaks, to reorganize his army, to draw reinforcements from the West, and finally to proceed to a junction with Jackson, and to the execution of a grand plan, which was calculated to deal a decisive blow to the main Union army.

In the middle of June the Rebel cavalry had made a reconnoissance in the rear of the Federal army; and toward the end of this month, when solid bridges over the Chickahominy had been constructed, an advance was determined on; but scarcely had it begun by the Union troops of the left wing, when the Rebels, consisting of Jackson, Hill, and Longstreet's corps, under General Lee, appeared on the right flank of the right wing of the Federal army, and proceeded immediately to the attack.

Taking the map in hand, it will be seen that by this movement the Rebels took hold at once of the communications of the Federal army, and that the right wing, once beaten, would be thrown against the Chickahominy with its swamps; while the left wing, shut up between Richmond and the Chickahominy, had scarcely any other chance than to surrender. The defeat of the right wing, therefore, would decide the destruction of the entire army of the Potomac. The conception of this plan was good, and worthy of a great general. The Union army, separated, and the most important wing exposed to the blows of a greatly superior force, seemed to be lost. This time, however, the defense was equal to the attack. James River was open to the Federal gun-boats, and by marching straight to it, on the right bank of the Chickahominy, leaving the main Rebel army on the left bank, the army might be saved. The Chickahominy was difficult to cross. The Rebels had passed over a bridge some 10 miles above the utmost right of the Union troops; if, therefore, the Federal army crosses on its own bridges, and destroys those behind it, the Rebels have to return by their bridge, and lose one day in useless marching, and this might be enough. Once near James River, the army could take shelter under the gun-boats. As soon, therefore, as the Rebels appear on the right flank, the right wing is ordered to oppose them, while the train is sent over the bridges to join the left wing. At the end of the second day the right wing was beaten, but the train had crossed, and, night coming on, a rout of the Union forces was prevented. The troops of the beaten wing then followed their train, crossed the creek, and destroyed the bridges behind them. The junction of the right and left wings took place, and the retreat toward James River was immediately commenced. This plan of defense reflects the highest credit and honor on the general who conceived and carried it out; and the entire operation of the defense, as well as of the attack, must be looked upon as two of the finest movements executed during the war.

History presents an example of a similar operation to that executed in the seven days' fight. In 1674, Montecuculi crossed the Rhine to attack Turenne on French soil; Turenne avoided the attack by himself crossing that river, and entering on German ground. Montecuculi was thereby forced to retreat, and recross the Rhine to defend his own country.

The fight at Gaines's Mill took place on the 27th, and on the 29th the Rebels had come back to the right bank and commenced the attack. The retreat was, nevertheless, continued, the Rebels following the retreating troops with the utmost determination. A rear guard, left after the crossing of White Oak Swamp, was attacked by them with great energy, and at Malvern Hill a final attempt was made to throw the whole army of the Potomac into James River. This determined pursuit was correct, and would probably have produced greater results had the distance been only one or two marches longer. The Potomac army had suffered severely in the retreat, and was greatly disorganized on its arrival at Malvern Hill and Harrison's Landing.

The only fault which seems to have been committed on the side of the Rebels was, that the attacks on the Union rear guards were not executed in sufficient force. How far they were adapted to the topography of the country, we are unable to judge. At Malvern Hill, for instance, it would appear that the dispositions for the attack were not in accordance with the ground, and were far from having been correct.

After the failure at Malvern Hill, the Rebels could not expect that another attack would succeed; and both armies being exhausted, a pause occurred in the operations. The position at Harrison's Landing threatened Richmond on both sides of the James River, as the Union army, by means of its gun-boats, commanded the river, and could cross it at will. This position of affairs obliged the Rebel army to retreat to the neighborhood of Richmond, so as to be able to act on either side, using Richmond as a double *tête-de-pont,* and acting against the Union army from whatever side it would advance.

After the troubles created by Jackson's offensive movement against General Banks, the armies of Generals McDowell, Fremont, and Banks were consolidated; General Burnside, with his troops, was called from Roanoke Island, and General Stevens's division from Port Royal. These troops were then ordered to Fredericksburg.

July passed without any event of importance. Jackson had moved to Gordonsville; and it was the 12th of August before the army of the Potomac, by commencing its retreat, gave the signal for another offensive movement on the part of the Rebels, not against this army, but in a northward direction, against the army of Virginia, then under command of General Pope.

Before passing this campaign in review, we must be permitted to say a few words on the previous inaction of the Rebels, which lasted from the commencement of July to the 12th of August.

In operations where an army holds a central position

between two hostile armies, the main chance of success lies in attacking one after the other, before they can unite, or before they can arrive so near as to make a simultaneous attack on the main body holding the central position. Great speed and immediate action are therefore necessary to obtain great results, and it is evident that the best moment to attack one of the two armies acting on exterior lines, is immediately after the defeat of the other, for the simple reason that the defeated army is not in a position, morally or physically, to take up the offensive for some time; besides, the enemy has no time to bring his armies to a junction or to reinforce or withdraw them; and finally, the moral effect of two victories, one gained directly after the other, is very great. In the present case, therefore, the Rebels, immediately after the Malvern Hill fight, ought to have moved north, leaving only 20,000 to 30,000 men at Richmond. Supposing they had taken three to four days to repose and reorganize their army, they might have been on the eighth or ninth day at Warrenton. Attacking the forces there with impetuosity, they would have beaten them, and, pursuing them from Warrenton to Washington in the same style they had pursued the Union army from the Chickahominy to James River, little doubt can be entertained that they would have completely routed them. Passing the Potomac a few miles above Washington, the capture of one or two forts on the left side of the river would have insured the capture of the town, and there would have been but few troops to oppose the Rebels in their attempt. The Potomac army, in its condition when at Harrison's Landing, could not and did not take the offensive during the first fortnight after its retreat; and the Rebel army once before Washington, it would have been very soon recalled to the defense of the Federal capital.

Several considerations may have influenced the long inactivity of the Rebels: one, that they thought the climate of Harrison's Landing would finish what the sword had commenced, and greatly reduce or destroy the Potomac army, without their doing anything for it; or they felt not strong enough to undertake this movement. This last reason, however, we cannot admit, for afterward they attacked the two Union armies united; besides, their strength may be computed about as follows: It has been stated that they had from 150,000 to 200,000 men engaged in the seven days' fight. This is certainly a great mistake. The main army under Lee, attacking the Federal right wing, numbered, according to the estimation and reports of Union generals, 60,000 men, which means that probably it amounted to not more than 50,000. The other part of the Rebel army was left on the defensive, or at least was not commanded by any general of renown. The Rebel army before Richmond had no other task than to defend that place and hold the Union left wing in check. This army, having a secondary part to play, was certainly not stronger than the main army. The whole, therefore, probably did not exceed 100,000 to 110,000 men. Of these, 15,000 to 20,000 were disabled in the seven days' fight; 20,000 were required for the defense of Richmond; hence 60,000 were left for the offensive movement; and this was fully sufficient, considering the strength of the army at Warrenton. If the presence of the army of the Potomac really did prevent the Rebels following a course similar to the one described above, then their inaction must be considered as a grave military fault, which probably was the first cause of their losing the campaign at the end.

As we have already stated, the departure of the army of the Potomac became the signal for an offensive movement against the army under General Pope, who had advanced to Culpepper, General Burnside's corps remaining meanwhile at Fredericksburg. On the 10th of August General Jackson had already encountered General Banks; but it was not till about the 20th that the advance of the whole Rebel army was felt; and then General Pope commenced his retreat. The Rebels, however, had delayed their movement too long. On the 20th of August General McClellan's army commenced disembarking at Aquia Creek to join Pope near Warrenton. On the 27th these troops were ordered to Manassas Junction to attack General Jackson, who had turned the right flank of the Union army, and had passed through Thoroughfare Gap, in the rear of the Federal troops. Generals Sigel and McDowell were ordered to Gainesville, to intercept communication between Jackson and Lee, but were subsequently sent to Manassas Junction. On the 28th and 29th the fight becomes general; the Federal army is defeated, retreats, is outflanked once more at Centreville, and takes shelter behind the fortifications of Washington on the 2d of September.

Let us consider first the attack. The object of the attack was evidently to defeat Pope before General McClellan's army could effect a junction with him. This was only possible by leaving Richmond before the army of the Potomac left Harrison's Landing. By not doing so, the object could evidently not be carried out; and the long inaction of the Rebel army was therefore, as already said, a fault.

The direction they gave to their line of operation was a sound and good one. Pope's front of operation was perpendicular to the Potomac; it was therefore the wing opposite the river which was to be attacked, and the whole army thrown against it. It is a general rule, that an army pointing with one wing to an unsurmountable obstacle and having the other wing in the air, is always to be attacked on this last wing, and to be pressed against the obstacle—a river, a swamp, a mountain, the sea, or whatever it may be—where it will be forced to surrender. This rule is one of the elementary rules of strategy; and the course the Confederate armies would take could therefore not be one moment doubtful. It was obvious that they would attack and turn the right wing of the Union army, and, after the slightest success was gained on this wing, they would push the army in the direction of the Potomac, and force it to surrender there. This was in fact the course followed by the Rebels, and they thereby rapidly conducted the Federal troops from the Rapidan to Washington.

As far as the details of the operation are concerned, we must confess that we know too little about them to form any precise opinion. One thing, however, seems clear, viz., that a division of the Confederate forces took place; and that while one part of them was amusing the Union army in front, another part marched in its rear. This division was evidently a mistake, and would have been paid for dearly by them had the first direction of Sigel's and McDowell's corps been followed up. We must, nevertheless, admit that the *direction* taken by Jackson's corps was admirably chosen, in complete harmony with the rules of strategy and with the natural features of the country; and the only objection we have to make is, that it was executed with part only, instead of with the entire force of the Rebels. If the simultaneous march of the whole Rebel army was impossible, it would perhaps have been more correct to fall on General Sigel's corps, which was near Waterloo, unsupported, in front of the Rebel army, and therefore exposed to their blows.

The way the flank movement was executed by the Rebels certainly deserves credit, if it is considered that it became known only when Jackson was already through Thoroughfare Gap—that is to say, entirely in the rear of the Union army. Besides the loss of time and the division of force, one more reproach may be made to the attack. It is, that the pursuit, after the battle, was not nearly so energetic as in the seven days' fight; and thereby the whole fruit of the victory was lost.

Though the attack, as we have seen, was not entirely correct, the defense was still less so. No advantage was taken of the mistakes of the Rebels; and in fact it was a series of the most serious military errors, as will be shown in the following dicussion.

When General Pope commenced his retreat, it was known that the whole Rebel army was moving against him. Only an immediate concentration of all the Union forces then in North Virginia, and those of McClellan's army coming from Yorktown, could save General Pope either from a defeat, or, at all events, from an inglorious retreat. Instead of such a concentration, we see General Pope at Culpepper; part of the Potomac army arriving at Aquia Creek, and marching toward Warrenton Junction; another part of the army of the Potomac transported to Alexandria, and remaining there; and finally, General Burnside staying with his corps at Fredericksburg. This looks very little like a concentration; and in fact General Pope was only joined by those corps which had moved from Aquia Creek to Warrenton Junction.

General Burnside's corps remained at Fredericksburg. What for, is more than difficult, it is impossible to say. Of what use was or could be the occupation of Fredericksburg? None. In fact, either the Rebels were victorious against Pope, then as a matter of course Fredericksburg could not have been held, as the troops there would have been certainly exposed to destruction; or the Rebels were beaten and thrown back south. In that case, Fredericksburg might have been at any moment occupied by the Union forces; and therefore there was no need of holding it, and depriving the Union troops of the succor of a whole corps.

By throwing into the scale, in the fights of the 29th and 30th, this and Banks's corps, which also did not participate, who knows but that these battles might have been won? At all events, a battle is so serious an affair that all chances should be calculated, and all possible efforts made to win it. To leave General Burnside's army on an utterly useless post, instead of engaging it on the decisive point, is violating the principal maxim of war, which is to concentrate the troops at the decisive moment and on the decisive point. This, however, is not all. Not only was this corps, against all rules, not engaged, but, against all rules, it was a detachment on an isolated post, where, exposed to the blows of a stronger enemy, it might at any moment have been crushed.

One reason only, for this, we believe, is alleged, at least such was the only reason presented to the Senate for the inaction of Burnside's corps, viz., that Fredericksburg was expected to serve as a base for some operations to be made afterward. It is not necessary to comment on such reasoning; it only proves, what we have already advanced on the subject, that the strategic importance of the different parts of the theater of war was very far from being understood. We have shown, in Chapters I., II., and III., that operations executed to the left of the main left zone cannot be decisive.

General Pope might, nevertheless, have obtained great results had this non-concentration been the only mistake; but another, perhaps quite as great a one, was made in the choice of the line of retreat. Once at Culpepper, and pressed by the Rebel army, General Pope had two lines of retreat open—one along the Culpepper and Manassas Railroad toward Alexandria, and the other from Culpepper to Markham, and thence to Knoxville and Berlin, on the Potomac. Two reasons recommended the choice of the latter line of retreat. The first is, that, as we have already said, the attack against the Union troops would be directed against their right wing, in obedience to elementary rules of strategy; and that the natural counter-movement would be, to move to the right to prevent being outflanked. Therefore, by moving to a position between Markham and Salem, the Union army would have avoided being outflanked, and would continually have presented its front instead of its flank to the attack. The next reason is, that by taking a position there, Washington was more effectually protected than by moving in a direct line to that place.

We will prove this. An army having to defend a certain point—an important town, for instance—may do so in two ways. One, by placing itself square before it, which is meanly defensive, and has, besides, the disadvantage that if the defending army is beaten, it is thrown pell-mell into the town with the pursuers; and consequently, instead of keeping the enemy off, this kind of defense really draws him to the object to be defended.

The other way to defend a point of importance is to take a flank position, *i.e.* such a position that the enemy, in order to attack the town, is obliged to offer his flank to the defending army. This way of defending is evidently offensive, and the only one a good general would choose, if the geography of the country allows it. In fact, the attacking army has, in this case, three lines of conduct open. Either to march straight to the object without heeding the defending army: this no general, of course, would dare to do, considering that he would offer his flank and rear to the defending army, which would avail itself of the occasion, and deal him a serious blow. Or to divide the army, masking with one part the defending army, and attacking the town with the other: this would give the defending army the chance of beating the attacking one in detail. Or finally, which is the only reasonable course, to march with the whole attacking army against the defending one. This, if not strong enough to accept battle, retreats, but marching away from the point of importance to defend, and thereby drawing the enemy away too, who cannot undertake anything against the town before having gained a decisive advantage over the defending army.

Applying this to our case, it will be seen, by taking the map in hand, that there are few cases where such a flanking position could have been more efficacious than in Eastern Virginia. If, for instance, the Federal army had taken a position along the Thoroughfare and Manassas Gap Railroad, and between these two places, holding Thoroughfare Gap, it would have been very soon in the flank and rear of any Rebel army advancing from the Rappahannock toward Washington, and this without any risk for its own communications.

If the Rebel army had, for example, advanced as far as Centreville, the Federal army, by debouching through Thoroughfare and Aldie Gaps, would have been on the flank, and on the communications of the Rebel army, which, if attacked and beaten, would have been thrown into the Potomac. To suppose that the Rebels would, nevertheless, choose so hazardous and wrong a course, would evidently be supposing that their generals were ignorant of the commonest rules of strategy; and this could scarcely be supposed, considering the signal proofs to the contrary they had already given.

Hence the correct line of retreat for General Pope's army would have been to Markham, Piedmont, etc., and if not strong enough to await an attack there, it ought to have continued its retreat and placed the Potomac between itself and the Rebels. The junction with the remainder of General McClellan's troops might have taken place at Knoxville and Berlin. Had this course been followed, what could the Rebels have done? Attack Washington on the right bank, with its thirty-five fortresses, and with General Pope's army on their left flank? Certainly not. Or cross the Potomac between Pope and Washington? Still more unlikely; utter destruction might have been the consequence. Or force the passage in front of General Pope? This would probably have been too difficult a task. There would, therefore, have been only one alternative left; this was to try to cross above General Pope by acting always to their left. This the Union army might have prevented by acting continually to the right. At all events, this course would have prevented the invasion of Maryland, the surrender of Harper's Ferry, and the useless butchery of Antietam. The Rebel army, in order to do anything, could only have acted in the direction opposite to Washington, and would thereby have receded from it, instead of nearing it or threatening it in the rear.

The retreat toward Washington was therefore a grave military fault, and it was aggravated by other mistakes, which were partly of a strategical, partly of a more tactical character; the accounts are, however, still so little cleared up, that we do not think it proper to enter into any further discussion of the subject. Let us merely notice two facts. The order sending Generals McDowell and Sigel to Gainesville to mask Thoroughfare Gap, and interpose between Jackson and Lee's forces, is certainly a luminous point in

the ensuing chaos. But this order ought to have been followed up by pushing all the other troops to the same point, and by advancing Sigel and McDowell on the Gainesville and Aldie Gap road. Instead of this, all the troops are drawn to the right, and the first manœuvre of the two generals became entirely useless, by marching them afterward to Manassas Junction and to Grovestown. To act correctly, Hooker, Kearney, and Porter ought to have been sent to Gainesville. Jackson would then have been really outflanked, and by moving the whole army rapidly forward in a northeasterly direction, he would finally have been thrown against Alexandria, where he would have been obliged to surrender. In the battle it would appear that the left wing was parellel to the Gainesville and Centreville Turnpike, pointing toward Thoroughfare Gap; evidently this wing was in the air, and exposed to the blows of reinforcements coming through the Gap, and, therefore, could not avoid being beaten. Another mistake committed in the battle, is the absence of General Banks's corps, whose movements or whereabouts are difficult to understand.

The next fact worthy of remark is the stay which the army made at Centreville, instead of retreating without delay to Washington, and moving thence immediately to Point of Rocks. Let us explain this somewhat more. The Rebels had driven General Pope at the point of the bayonet rapidly and violently from the Rapidan to Centreville. It could not be supposed that, after their victory at Manassas, they would remain idle; and the very simple question arises, what would or what could they do? Pope's army being at Centreville, they could attack him once more; if the position was too strong in front of the Union troops, the Rebels might outflank it again—as in fact they did. This latter being the safest and most decisive course the Rebels could adopt, no doubt could for an instant exist that they would adopt it. Staying at Centreville, therefore, was exposing the army to disaster, besides losing valuable time. Once outflanked at Centreville, the army had to come back at all events, and must be considered very lucky in being able to do so. After this retreat to Washington, what was the next thing the Rebels could do? To attack the thirty-five forts on the right bank of the Potomac, we have already said, would have been simply foolish; it was therefore out of the question. That they would remain idle, could not be supposed either; the only course left to them was to pass the Potomac, and the only question difficult to answer would seem to be—Where? Taking the map in hand, it will be seen that by crossing this river above Washington, the Rebels might at any time have prevented the Union army from retreating north, and would have shut it up in the Federal capital, cutting off all communications by land with the Northern States, and having only the communication by sea open. This manœuvre would, therefore, be a decisive one, if in the battle which would surely follow, the Union army should be thrown back into the town. What we advance evidently implies that the Union army is on the Potomac below where the Rebel army crosses—that is, between this army and the Chesapeake Bay. The very moment the Rebel army would cross, having the Union army above it, the manœuvre would become destructive to them, as they would, in case of defeat, be thrown against the fortifications of Washington or Chesapeake Bay, where they would obviously be obliged to surrender. Hence the Rebels could cross only above the Federal army; and this latter, by marching immediately from Manassas to Point of Rocks, the principal point where the roads from Manassas and Centreville lead to, the crossing of the Rebel army would have been hindered. It seems easy to reason in this way after the facts have transpired, and to stigmatize as a great military fault the non-execution of a manœuvre which, it might be said, was difficult to foretell. Such an objection would not, however, be applicable to me; those who will take the trouble to read the first chapter of my "Summary of the Art of War," written at the end of December, 1861,—that is to say, eight months before the events,—will find the very same remarks, only more fully developed; they will also find it expressly laid down, that after the defeat of the Union troops in Northern Virginia, Point of Rocks becomes the decisive point. Events having so clearly proved the truth of my reasoning of a year since, I am now certainly justified in calling the not sending of troops to Point of Rocks, to prevent the passage of the Rebels, a military fault.

We have said above, that after this successful Virginia campaign no other alternative was left to the Rebels but to invade Maryland. But here difficulties and considerations arose which it is interesting to investigate somewhat more closely. An invasion must have an object, and what could be the object of the Maryland campaign? From a really military point of view only one answer seems possible, viz., to gain possession of the communications of the

Union army at Washington, and to fight the decisive battle of the war—decisive for the North, and accompanied with little risk to themselves. If this was the object, and it was grand enough to justify the attempt, the Rebel army, instead of crossing at Point of Rocks, ought to have crossed between Rushville and Coon's Ferry, at which place they might have been by the first of September, in the evening, at the same instant that part of their troops attacked Pope in the rear near Fairfax C. H. On the morning of the second—that is to say, before even Pope was back at Alexandria—part of their forces might have been before Washington, on the left bank of the Potomac, and made a bold attempt to carry by surprise and escalade one or two of the forts on the left side. Had this coup-de-main been crowned with success, the way to Washington would have been laid wide open. Little danger accompanied such an attempt. Pope's army was at that time too disorganized to act offensively against the communications of the Rebels; besides, the terror in Washington would have been such that nobody would have thought of it; and at the very worst, the Rebels might have retreated to Point of Rocks or Sharpsburg. This course would probably have been the only admissible one, had Pope's army experienced a more serious defeat, amounting almost to destruction. Under the circumstances, it was probably thought that such an operation would be too adventurous and too risky; the consequence was, that a kind of middle course was followed, which leaves on the mind the impression of indecision, and which certainly was the cause of their losing the campaign. It is therefore difficult to say whether they intended first to fight the decisive battle on the

Monocacy, whether they only afterward determined on the operation against Harper's Ferry, or whether, as a general thing, they did not feel strong enough to fight the battle offensively, and preferred to fight it defensively with offensive return on ground chosen by them. There was a certain delay and wavering in their operations, which indicate indecision, and which lasted until finally the rapidly changing circumstances enforced a decision which was probably not the best they might have chosen. In short, the operations seem to indicate that at the moment the Rebels entered Maryland, they had no thoroughly studied plan of action, and no definite object in view; at least no one which was worth the risking of their main army for. Subsequently the defeated Union army had time to reorganize, to recover, to reinforce, and to reassume the offensive in a few days. The great maxim, "strike an enemy before he is prepared," was certainly left out of sight by the Rebels in this part of their offensive operation.

To show that what we advance is a fact, we need only follow the operations after the 1st of September. On the 5th the Rebels crossed the Potomac at Point of Rocks, and marched to Fredericktown. Thence to Hagerstown is one or two days' march. The investment on the south and west side of Harper's Ferry could be made from Leesburg by marching through Vestal's Gap, or about one day's march; taking two marches more to make a junction, by way of Martinsburg or Shepherdstown, between the forces coming from Hagerstown and those from Vestal's Gap, the investing of Harper's Ferry might have been completed on the 8th or the 9th, and, by an energetic action, the surrender might have been forced on the 10th or the 11th; instead of which four or five days are lost, for Harper's Ferry surrendered only on the 15th. This delay forced the Rebel army, on the 14th, to the two fights at Crampton's Gap and South Mountain, in order to gain time for the reduction of Harper's Ferry. These engagements cost a large number of men, and certainly must have somewhat demoralized their troops. Having finished their operations against Harper's Ferry, they immediately offer battle; but the circumstances and the strategical position of the army were already so changed that this battle could no longer have had the effect of a battle fought near the Monocacy or near Washington; and as one object—viz., the surrender of Harper's Ferry and the capture of 12,000 men—was accomplished, they might have dispensed with the battle, the more so as the field they chose for the battle-ground was only adapted for a defensive battle, and could not possibly be used for an offensive one. The result of defensive battles is in most cases but an insufficient one, as it can only have for effect the repulse, but never the total defeat and destruction of the enemy's army. The energy that both parties displayed during the last days of the Maryland campaign, and the determination with which they fought in the battle of Antietam, is highly creditable to both of them. I believe, however, it would have been more correct for the Rebels to cross the Potomac and fight the battle on the other side, the more so, as their position at Sharpsburg was a very dangerous one. Once defeated, disasters would certainly have been the consequence, having, as they had, the Potomac behind them. Their withdrawal from the left bank, in the night of the 18th, was well managed.

The defense, or, as it afterward turned out to be, the attack, in this campaign was somewhat better; at least it had a definite object—the driving of the Rebels out of Maryland, wherever they were to be found. This object was attained. Nevertheless, more might have been gained had it not been for some mistakes. The army of the Potomac took seven days to march from Washington to Fredericktown, a distance of 40 miles, or, at the outside, two days' march. This slowness evidently gave the Rebels the necessary time to complete their operations against Harper's Ferry. From Fredericktown the movement was conducted with more energy. The fights of South Mountain and Crampton Gap are creditable to the victors. The battle of Antietam was fought, and, though at one time a drawn battle, it became a victory in the result. The partial attempt to cross the river in pursuit of the Rebels was evidently a blunder, as it was plainly their intention to renew the battle at once, if it could only be done on their own terms—that is to say, in a position more advantageous to them than that of Sharpsburg, with the Potomac in their rear.

The inaction of the Federal army after the battle must also be considered as a fault. This army ought to have at once operated by way of Harper's Ferry, so as to act on the communications of the Rebels and force them to another fight, which might have been disastrous to them. The lesson the Rebels had given to the Federals in their Virginia campaign might have been made available against them, instead of letting them quietly retreat to Winchester.

The great and main fault committed in this short campaign was, however, the exposing of the troops at Harper's Ferry to capture. We have had repeated occasion to give our opinion on sending detachments to the rear of a stronger enemy. We have stated that they are against the rules of grand warfare, and that in most cases they turn out badly for those who make them, instead of for those against whom they are intended. Here is one of those cases. What was the use of holding Harper's Ferry the moment the Rebels were in Maryland and occupied Fredericktown? The place in itself has no importance. As a strategic point, it was only of importance against an enemy coming from Winchester, serving in this case as a kind of *tête-de-pont* for Union troops to debouch in the Shenandoah valley; besides, the garrison was sufficiently strong to prevent smaller corps of the enemy from crossing above and making raids into Maryland. By holding it, the Rebels could not be prevented from returning into Virginia, as in fact their main army did not return this way. The roads to Sharpsburg and Hagerstown were open, and no obstacle existed to prevent a recrossing near Berlin and Knoxville. Was it to save a few rounds of ammunition and cannon, that orders were given to hold the place? Why it was, we are at a loss to guess, unless it was that one of those schemes, which were such favorites with the old Spanish generals, was based upon it: that it was supposed that the men of Pennsylvania would occupy Williamsport, that Miles would hold Harper's Ferry, and that McClellan would push in the rear; perhaps the road by way of Sharpsburg was overlooked, and it was supposed that the Rebels would not do otherwise than surrender.

Harper's Ferry, as we have said, being of no importance

the moment the Rebels entered Maryland, the corps of Miles ought to have been ordered to retreat immediately by way of Sharpsburg and Williamsport, or Sharpsburg, Shepherdstown, Martinsburg, Hancock, or any other northeasterly route, unless the place was fortified and really defensible for a certain length of time against an army investing it on all sides. If the place was not defensible against an enemy coming from Maryland, the leaving of this detachment at Harper's Ferry must be considered as the most wanton and unmilitary sacrifice of men that was made during the campaign. We are going to show that the place was not defensible, and that nothing but utter ignorance of the topography of the country or of the rules of grand tactics can assert that it was.

The opposite cut gives the main features of the topography of the country. It will be seen by it that Maryland and Loudon Heights are two long mountain chains, which are prolongations of the Blue Ridge Mountains, separated from each other by the Potomac; both fall nearly vertically upon the river, leaving only space for a road on each side. The Shenandoah passes along Loudon Heights, and separates them from the town of Harper's Ferry and a kind of bluff called Bolivar Heights. The inclination of this bluff toward Harper's Ferry is gentle, but against the Virginia side very steep; Loudon and Maryland Heights overlook it considerably. The Potomac, about a mile or a mile and a half above Harper's Ferry, turns to the north, and the space between Maryland Heights and the river is filled up by a kind of table-land overlooking the incline of Bolivar Heights, and falling also vertically, or very nearly so, toward the Po-

Fig. 7.

Maryland heights
Potomac
Bolivar heights
Loudon heights
Shenandoah
a'
A'
B'
b'
a
A
b

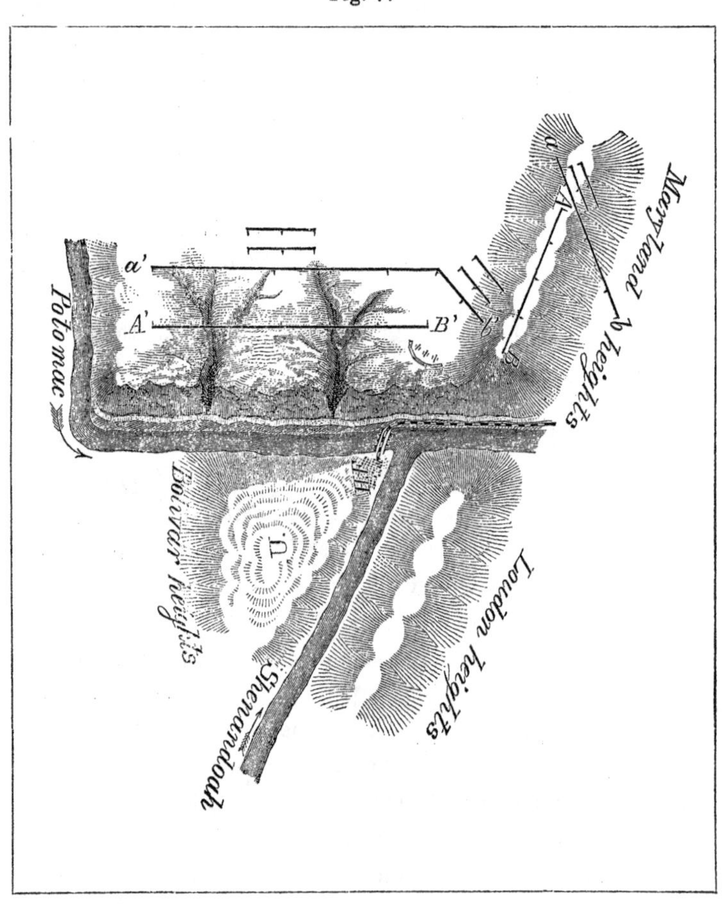

tomac. The camp of the garrison was on the incline of Bolivar Heights, at *U*. From Loudon Heights this space could be battered directly; and from Maryland Heights, or the table-land on the Maryland side, it could be enfiladed. Maryland and Loudon Heights were wooded, and on a small, open space on the table-land at *C* was placed a battery of a few heavy pieces, pointing toward Bolivar Heights. No intrenchments of any description could be discovered on Maryland or Loudon Heights. From this sketch it will be understood that the party holding these two mountain chains was evidently master of the battery, and consequently of Harper's Ferry and Bolivar Heights.

Col. Miles's orders were, I believe, to hold Harper's Ferry, by occupying Maryland Heights in force. Now, considering the topography of the country, he could occupy Maryland Heights only by forming a line of battle like *A B*, or like *A′ B′*. Both positions are so entirely against all military rules, that no general would ever attempt to fight a battle in a similar array, as in both cases his defeat would be inevitable, and accompanied with the most severe loss, with no benefit whatever to the cause he is fighting for. The reason is easy to perceive. An army (*A B*) along the mountain crest has one wing leaning against a precipice; the other wing would be attacked by an army formed in oblique line of battle, like *a b*; and as the attack would evidently dispose of more men, *A B* would be thrown over the precipice. The army *A′ B′* has the precipice in its rear, and therefore the slightest advantage gained against any point of its position would be the ruin of the whole corps.

It is useless to say much about such positions. Those who are willing to read from authorities what we have just advanced, may take up Jomini, Baron de Ternay, or any good work on grand tactics. A battle fought under such circumstances would last five or six hours, and terminate with the destruction of the whole corps.

What could the commander of Harper's Ferry do under similar circumstances? To act according to his orders and fight a battle on Maryland or Loudon Heights was sacrificing a large number of men without an object; to stay at Bolivar Heights was impossible. Only two courses were, therefore, left open: either to surrender, or to open a way with the bayonet in the direction of Martinsburg. The latter course was evidently the more honorable, and the only one becoming a true soldier; if repulsed, there was always time to surrender, and the honor of the flag would have been saved.

Before passing in review the last part of the campaign, we will say a few words respecting the offensive operations of the Rebels on the whole theater of war, considered as one great plan of attack.

Simultaneously with the movement against Pope, those against Buell and Grant were executed. The entire plan was based on an action on interior lines of all the Rebel armies, and the direction of all the movements was sound and good. The only mistake (and it was a great one) was, that all these operations were simultaneous, instead of being consecutive; 50,000 more men in the East, or 50,000 more in the West, would have obtained decisive results. The campaign of 1800 was studied, but not thoroughly. Napoleon, in that campaign, only invaded Italy after Moreau had obtained decisive results on the Rhine, and could send him a reinforcement of 15,000 men.

We have seen that after the battle of Antietam another long pause in the operations took place. The Rebels had retreated to Winchester; had been reinforced, and reorganized and recovered themselves there; and being on the defensive, quietly awaited the next movement of the Union army. This movement finally took place at the commencement of November. The Union army marched down Loudon valley, and went in this direction as far as Waterloo and Warrenton. There General McClellan was relieved; and with the change of command, probably a change in the plan of operation took place; for after a stay of eight days at or near Warrenton, the army marched to Fredericksburg. There it gave the enemy full time to prepare and concentrate. On the 12th of December it crossed the river; on the 13th it attacked the Rebel position, and, being repulsed with loss, recrossed to the other side.

We do not know, and can only with difficulty surmise, the object of this campaign. Probably it was the remote, final capture of Richmond. The object was certainly not to beat or to destroy the Rebel army, as the Federal army advanced without paying the slightest attention to this army stationed at Winchester, which, in fact, had to run after the Union army to get a fight out of it at Fredericksburg.

We have already said that the main object of the Union army ought to be the destruction of the Rebel army, and not the capture of a town, or a small tract of land. The object which evidently formed the basis of the whole plan of operation being not well considered, the plan itself could not be well studied, or be according to the maxims of war.

What was this plan of operation? Was it to move down the army to Gordonsville, and thence to Richmond, stealing itself between this town and the Rebel army, and snatching the long-coveted prize away from the latter? By going to Fredericksburg, was the idea the same, but the route changed? And this, all the time with the Rebel army in the flank or rear! But perhaps it was thought this army would stay idle at Winchester! Doubtless, Dumourier's invasion of Holland in 1793, and Pichegru's movement in Belgium in 1794, must have served as models for this campaign. I prefer referring to Jomini's "Summary of the Art of War," and his "Wars of the Revolution." The reader will find there the question more thoroughly treated than I am able to treat it; and as Jomini is a great military authority, his judgment on the case will have more weight than mine.

Once at Fredericksburg, the Rappahannock was to be crossed, in order to move forward. This river, which near Waterloo (where the army was before moving to Fredericksburg) did not measure more than ten yards in width, is a considerable stream near Fredericksburg, and consequently the first difficulties ensued. It took a considerable time to procure pontoons. Meanwhile the Rebels, as if entirely sure that they would be attacked in front, made all necessary arrangements to repulse such an attack.

To understand this battle fully, the reader may suppose a plain, about a mile to a mile and a half wide, bordered on each side by a range of hills, about one hundred feet high. The northern range of hills was occupied by the Union army, and close to the foot of these hills is the Rappahannock. The southern range of hills was occupied by the Southern army. About two miles above Fredericksburg, the southern range of hills forms a large curve, and comes close to the river, forming thereby a kind of semicircle around the town. The plain between the two armies was commanded by the guns of either army; and Fredericksburg being close to the river, was evidently commanded entirely by Northern guns. Consequently the crossing would be attended with no serious difficulty; and for the same reason, the recrossing or withdrawing of the army could be done without danger.

Either of the two armies entering the plain between the two ranges of hills would be destroyed by the artillery of the opposite party. The Union army attempted it, and paid dearly for it. Had the Rebels tried to follow up their victory, they would have experienced the same fate that the Federal army did in attempting the attack.

Considering this state of affairs, it was obviously a mistake to cross in front; the more so, as the simple crossing a few miles above would have carried the position. And had this operation been well and secretly conducted, as it ought to be done in similar cases, the Rebels would have been obliged to sacrifice a rear guard, in order to save their army. In fact, the Rebel right wing pointed toward the

Potomac or York River. The elementary rule of strategy, already mentioned several times, wills therefore that the attack should have been directed against the Rebel left wing.

With the battle of Fredericksburg the campaign ends, and we wish only to say a few words by way of conclusion.

In the Union plan of invasion, the first and main object of the campaign was misunderstood. Occupation was taken for this object, instead of the beating and destroying of the Rebel armies. The consequence of this mistake was the formation of a great number of lines of operation. Hence division of force; hence defeats and retreats.

The facilities offered by the navy—by sea and river gun-boats—had the most deteriorating effect on the operations. It was almost taken for granted that without them operations were impossible, and with them irresistible. The consequence of this gun-boat mania was, and is still, that the best lines of communication, but the least decisive lines of operation, were invariably chosen. The large rivers on the sea-coast attracted the Union generals like magnets. If ever a circumstance conducts them into the interior of the country, immediately these rivers, and the thought of safety and gun-boats, draw them back.

As far as gun-boats are concerned, they ought to play a very secondary part—merely to serve as a kind of diversion, but never to intrust large operations to, or confine to their guns the safety of a large army, as was done at Shiloh and Harrison's Landing. Of how little use gun-boats are in really grand operations, may be seen from the fact that, as a general rule, the Rebels had none, and nevertheless were able to defeat us in several campaigns, though we had many.

The Rebel operations, looked at as a whole, were much sounder, and more according to the maxims of grand war. The direction of their lines of operation was, in most cases, decisive; but accidents, or the defective organization of volunteer armies, deprived them of the full results. The only reproach that can be made to their defense is, that it might have been somewhat grander—by giving up more on one side, but gaining more on the other—*i.e.* by concentrating still more to gain more decisive results.

The study of the campaign of 1796, wherein Napoleon gave up his whole siege-park, in order to regain it afterward, and the study of the campaign of 1800, had not been made thoroughly.

We close here our review of the campaign of 1862. We must repeat once more that we do not wish to have it considered as a historical, and still less, as a kind of political review. We have simply taken facts, belonging already to the public, as we found them, and have formed from them the text of a purely military treatise. Should we have committed errors in the narration of the facts, it must be excused. The object of this work is a purely scientific one, and the fault in the narration is of no importance, if the discussion of the wrongly-stated fact, as we give it, be but correct.

Finally, we must say that we do not at all wish this discussion to be considered personal, or directed against any one general in particular. Such an idea is foreign to our purpose; the more so, as the views we have set forth in this treatise are far from being generally adopted. English, French, and German writers, for instance, differ widely on the subject; and the question, how different wars ought best to be conducted, is still a mooted question. Besides, many things in the present war have been entirely new, or different from what takes place in Europe. The entire absence of a highly-educated general staff corps; the organization of volunteer armies; the want of correct and good maps; the difficulty of obtaining information; and the scarcity of provisions in many districts, are so many excuses for movements which, viewed merely from the stand-point of science, would be considered as mistakes.

# V.

## CAMPAIGN OF 1863.

In passing in review the campaign of 1862, we have seen how a wrong general plan, a division of force, a choice of indecisive lines of operation, led to insignificant results, and even reverses. The campaign of 1863 opens for the Union forces without any change in the general plan of operation; it is but the continuation of the campaign of 1862. The capture of Richmond and the opening of the Mississippi seem still to be the main objects to be obtained by the Eastern and Western Union armies.

A wrong general plan of operation will lead to bad or insignificant results even if the counter-plan be correct, whatever the minor or detailed operations may be. In the plan of 1863, probably these latter will be different from those of 1862; but nevertheless the result ought to be the same.

A long study of military history has led me to the conviction that great decisive results can only be obtained by a thoroughly correct action, especially in a case like ours, where the adversary is a skillful one, and understands the great rules of war himself, and, what is of more importance, knows how to apply them.

We have shown, in Chapters I., II., and IV., that great wars of conquest or invasion, conducted on a number of lines of operation, concentric toward the interior of the country, are against the rules laid down for such wars. The campaign of 1862 as well as that of 1863 are conducted on a great number of lines of operation, and consequently on wrong principles. Moreover, the general plan of operation being wrong, the objects which are to be attained by the different armies are such that, even were the plan of operation right, nothing decisive could be achieved.

Similar assertions are generally answered by the arguments, that in this country the distances are too great; that the extent of territory is too vast, and consequently war of conquest is out of the question; that peace can only be enforced by occupying all the principal towns of the South, and by opening all the rivers; that the Confederate States will meanwhile exhaust themselves, and are already very much exhausted; that nearly all their means are used up; that the North possesses now an irresistible superiority; and that a few large battles more, even if not decisive, will so weaken the Southern armies that they will not be able to do much more mischief.

It may be that all this is true; and that, in fact, the whole rebellion will break down quite as suddenly as it rose up. Considered, however, from a purely military point of view, I entertain some doubts as to the soundness of the above reasoning. By closely examining the theater of war, the strength and position of the two contending armies, and by drawing the correct defense according to the rules of grand war, it will be seen that the South, by making a last effort, might come victorious out of a struggle which should have lasted but a short time, were the intrinsic strength of both parties alone to be considered. I will draw this correct defense as well as I am able; and the reader may then judge for himself if my doubts of the above-mentioned reasoning are justified or not.

I have added a map, showing the approximative position of the contending armies, and giving also the principal lines of operation, for our imaginary campaign. The following table exhibits the strength of the two contending parties respectively, as well as I could judge from the different newspaper reports. Very likely these figures are not entirely correct, or rather most of them are probably incorrect. This is, however, of little importance, as it does in no way alter the principle in the matter; and I shall therefore suppose them to be correct:—

UNION FORCES.

| | | | |
|---|---|---|---|
| Army of | the Potomac | 140,000 | men. |
| " | Washington | 60,000 | " |
| " | Baltimore | 15,000 | " |
| " | Harper's Ferry, Maryland, and Potomac | 10,000 | " |
| " | Winchester | 5,000 | " |
| " | Fortress Monroe | 10,000 | " |
| " | Yorktown, Suffolk, and Norfolk | 20,000 | " |
| " | Newbern | 50,000 | " |
| " | Port Royal | 20,000 | " |
| " | New Orleans and Baton Rouge | 20,000 | " |
| " | Vicksburg | 60,000 | " |
| " | Helena | 5,000 | " |
| " | Memphis | 10,000 | " |
| " | Corinth | 20,000 | " |
| " | Bolivar | 15,000 | " |
| " | Jackson | 5,000 | " |
| " | Columbus | 5,000 | " |
| " | Missouri and Arkansas | 50,000 | " |
| " | Nashville | 10,000 | " |
| " | Murfreesborough | 40,000 | " |
| " | Kentucky | 40,000 | " |
| Detachments, etc. | | 40,000 | " |
| | Grand total | 650,000 | " |

CONFEDERATE FORCES.

| | |
|---|---|
| Army of Virginia | 120,000 men. |
| " Richmond | 20,000 " |
| " Petersburg | 5,000 " |
| " Blackwater | 5,000 " |
| " Newbern | 5,000 " |
| " Charleston | 15,000 " |
| " Savannah | 15,000 " |
| " Tullahoma | 50,000 " |
| " Vicksburg | 50,000 " |
| " Mobile | 10,000 " |
| " Arkansas | 15,000 " |
| Detachments, etc | 20,000 " |
| Grand total | 330,000 " |

The disparity of forces is enormous, according to these two tables; perhaps, in fact, it is not so great. This would, however, in our case, only aggravate the matter, as then the defense would have evidently still greater advantage.

The above numbers are such that obviously the South cannot afford to make blunders; and were their system of defense based on as vicious a plan as our attack, the war would evidently be soon finished, as in such a case the mere numbers would tell.

Those who have made a special study of military history will have found that a great difference exists even between plans considered correct. A plan of attack or defense may be correct without being grand; more or less knowledge, more or less genius, may be shown in it. Who, for instance, would doubt that a Napoleon would have dealt differently with Jourdan and Moreau in 1796, had he been in the place of the Archduke Charles, though the latter's campaign against the two French generals was not only correct, but is even considered as a model of a defensive campaign? Who could blame the general for refusing to fight a battle under exactly the same circumstances Napoleon did at Rivoli? He might have retreated, and it would have been correct; but to fight the battle was both correct and grand.

In a similar way, the defense of the South might be correct, without being grand or displaying genius; and though they would, in such a case, probably obtain sufficient results, I believe that the whole nature of the contest requires a somewhat greater effort than strict correctness. A kind of methodic war would drag on in length, and this the South will certainly have to avoid.

Correct, but audacious, and perhaps even somewhat adventurous, operations alone can obtain brilliant successes; and the war, as we understand it, for the South is that of Napoleon's campaign in 1796, only on a larger scale. Giving up everything, except the place where the army stands; concentrating their entire force on the decisive point; being victorious there; and gaining, by a few well-directed blows, not only what has been lost, but more too, is the lesson we may derive from this admirable campaign.

It is based on such reflections, and on the conviction that really decisive results on one point can only be obtained by a large superiority of force, that I shall sketch the defense. Besides, as the Confederate States have, like Europe, adopted the system of conscription, I will suppose that they have also introduced the system of keeping always the *cadres* of regiments or brigades full by new recruits. By supposing this, I avoid the necessity of making a reduction of numbers after every one of our imaginary battles.

Moreover, I shall be obliged, in some of the operations, to give a great number of details concerning the concentration of troops: first, to show how, as a general matter, such concentration should be executed; and secondly, to justify to a certain extent my reasoning, which, without these details, might appear in some cases extravagant.

The object of the South in making war is to repel invasion, and to enforce peace and their recognition. These objects can only be attained by destroying some of the principal Union armies and by taking the Federal capital; then making peace with the Federal Government, or with the different States separately, by threatening them with invasion. The first object, or the main object of the campaign, is therefore the destruction of the Union armies, or part of them.

Taking the map in hand, it will be seen—

1. That the Union forces are scattered over a large tract of land.

2. That they are acting on exterior lines.

3. That the Rebel forces are acting on interior lines.

Consequently the natural plan of operation, in such a state of things, is to concentrate on the different points successively, and to defeat the Union troops successively and in detail, *i.e.* before they can unite. In campaigns of this description, the principle is to make a break, generally in the center of the long front of operation, thereby preventing the junction of the two wings, and then to defeat these separately. In our present case it is difficult to say where the center of the front of operation is, considering that the Union forces have a front of operation from Port Royal to Washington, another from Washington to Memphis, and another from Memphis to New Orleans. At any point, therefore, where the Rebels attack the Union forces, they could make a breach, except on the two extremities, New Orleans and Port Royal. Now, evidently the points where they might break through are of very different relative importance. We have already contended that the left zone is the most important and the most decisive: the main blow ought, therefore, to be struck there. The principal Union armies are, however, of such strength in it, that it would require a concentration of nearly the whole Confederate forces to obtain decisive results against those armies. Having, in consequence of such a concentration, no Rebel armies opposed to them, the Federal armies in the West could destroy too much property—just now of great value to the Rebels—and could, besides, send immediate and enormous reinforcements to the East; and in this case, the whole advantage which the present position of the Union armies offers to the Confederate forces would be lost. It is therefore clear that, before attacking the main Union army in the left zone—that is, before coming to the last decisive struggle—the road ought to be well prepared by crushing all the smaller armies in the East and those in the Northwest—that is to say, by destroying the Union forces in Kentucky and Tennessee, and thereby breaking the connecting link between East and West. This would place all the Western Union armies on the defensive, and would give the Confederate forces time to prepare for the main or decisive campaign in the left zone.

Looking at the map, it will be seen that two armies—one

in the East, the Union army at Newbern, and one in the West, the Union army at Murfreesborough—are excellently posted for the Rebels to open the campaign by two decisive blows. The army at Newbern especially ought to be attacked: first, because it is a large detachment greatly exposed; and secondly, because it threatens continually one of the principal lines of communication of the South between the East and West.

To make successful attacks, concentration of troops is requisite, and to strike decisive blows, those concentrations should be so directed that the enemy shall not be apprised of them till it is too late. To concentrate troops slowly, *vis-à-vis* to an enemy, is always a great mistake. He has time to reinforce himself, or to take other steps to prevent disasters. We can only point, in order to show how concentrations ought to be effected, to the miraculous concentrations executed by Napoleon in his campaign of 1806, near Bamberg; in 1812, in Russia; and in 1815, near Charleroi, in Belgium. His columns, coming from all directions, marching 25 miles a day, arrived on one and the same day at the designated spot of rendezvous. It was always at this day of concentration, and never sooner, that Napoleon himself joined the army, and immediately put it in motion against the enemy. In 1806, the concentration and forward movement of Napoleon had been so rapid, that the Prussian commanders could scarcely credit the fact till they found themselves in front of his army. Just as great a mistake would it be to send a commander of reputation to effect a junction with another army, and that he should arrive before his troops did. His name is generally sufficient to give ample proof that his corps is following; therefore, commanders of corps as well as the commander-in-chief should arrive only on the same day—that is to say, the day when the whole army concentrates, coming from all sides to the rendezvous. It is obvious that the offensive operations have to commence at once, and to be carried out with the utmost rapidity. Without this, the effect gained by this sudden concentration would be entirely lost.

The Union army at Newbern we have supposed to be 50,000 men strong. The concentration of Confederate forces to destroy them might be conducted in the following way:—

| | | |
|---|---|---|
| Already near Newbern | 5,000 | men. |
| From Savannah | 10,000 | " |
| " Charleston | 10,000 | " |
| " Richmond | 15,000 | " |
| " Army of Virginia | 33,000 | " |
| " Blackwater | 3,000 | " |
| " Petersburg | 4,000 | " |
| Total | 80,000 | " |

These troops start from their respective whereabouts, and arrive all on one and the same day at Goldsborough. To render the understanding of the movements easy, we will commence counting with the 1st of month 1, and go on counting month 2, 3, etc.

For the movement of the above troops railroads may be used to a great extent. I suppose that generally those roads are able to convey 2500 men a day, with the exception of the shorter distances—from Fredericksburg to Richmond, for instance, or from Richmond to Petersburg. The following tables will show the complete movement:—

| Men. | Start by railroad from— | For— | Month 1. | Arrive at— | Month 1. |
|---|---|---|---|---|---|
| 11,000 | Fredericksburg | Richmond | 1st | Richmond | 1st. |
| 11,000 | Fredericksburg | Richmond | 2d | Richmond | 2d. |
| 11,000 | Fredericksburg | Richmond | 3d | Richmond | 3d. |
| 5,000 | Richmond | Burkesville | 2d | Burkesville | 2d. |
| 6,000 | Richmond | Petersburg | 2d | Petersburg | 2d. |
| 5,000 | Richmond | Richmond C. H. | 3d | Richmond C. H. | 3d. |
| 6,000 | Richmond | Hicksford | 3d | Hicksford | 3d. |
| 5,000 | Richmond | Richmond C. H. | 4th | Richmond C. H. | 4th. |
| 6,000 | Richmond | Weldon | 4th | Weldon | 4th. |
| 10,000 | Savannah | Charleston, by lots of 2500. | 2d, 3d, 4th, and 5th. | Charleston | 2d, 3d, 4th, and 5th. |
| 2,500 | Charleston | Cheraw | 2d | Cheraw | 2d. |
| 2,500 | Charleston | Whitesville | 3d | Whitesville | 3d. |
| 2,500 | Charleston | Wilmington | 4th | Wilmington | 4th. |
| 2,500 | Charleston | Washington, N. C | 5th | Washington, N. C | 5th. |
| 2,500 | Charleston | Hillsborough | 2d | Hillsborough | 3d. |
| 2,500 | Charleston | Raleigh | 3d | Raleigh | 4th. |
| 2,500 | Charleston | Smithfield | 4th | Smithfield | 5th. |
| 2,500 | Charleston | Smithfield | 5th | Smithfield | 6th. |

| Men. | March from— | Month 1. | For— | Time. | Arrive at— | Month 1. |
|---|---|---|---|---|---|---|
| 5,000 | Burkesville | 3d | Goldsborough | 7 days' march | Goldsborough | 9th. |
| 6,000 | Petersburg | 3d | Goldsborough | 7 days | Goldsborough | 9th. |
| 5,000 | Richmond C. H. | 4th | Goldsborough | 6 days | Goldsborough | 9th. |
| 6,000 | Hicksford | 4th | Goldsborough | 6 small do | Goldsborough | 9th. |
| 5,000 | Richmond C. H. | 5th | Goldsborough | 5 forced do* | Goldsborough | 9th. |
| 6,000 | Weldon | 5th | Goldsborough | 5 small do | Goldsborough | 9th. |
| 15,000 | Richmond | 1st | Goldsborough | 9 days | Goldsborough | 9th. |
| 2,500 | Cheraw | 3d | Goldsborough | 6 days | Goldsborough | 9th. |
| 2,500 | Hillsborough | 4th | Goldsborough | 5 days | Goldsborough | 9th. |
| 2,500 | Whitesville | 4th | Goldsborough | 5 days | Goldsborough | 9th. |
| 2,500 | Raleigh | 5th | Goldsborough | 4 small do | Goldsborough | 9th. |
| 5,000 | Smithfield | 8th | Goldsborough | 1 day | Goldsborough | 9th. |
| 2,500 | Wilmington | 5th | Goldsborough | 4 days | Goldsborough | 9th. |
| 2,500 | Washington, N. C | 6th | Goldsborough | 3 days | Goldsborough | 9th. |
| 5,000 | At Goldsborough. | | | | | |
| 80,000 | | | | | | |

* These troops should arrive in the night, from 4th to 5th, at Richmond C. H., so as to enable them to march on the 5th, when they will have 6 days, instead of 5.

On one and the same day 80,000 men would therefore march into Goldsborough; and if also the Union commander would be informed of the fact that reinforcements have arrived there, he would never know how many, and would certainly never think that 80,000 could arrive at the same moment.

This operation is evidently a main operation, and ought therefore to be conducted by the general-in-chief himself of the Rebel army. Starting in the night of the 8th or 9th from Fredericksburg or Richmond, he would arrive at the same time with the army, and could prepare everything for the offensive movement to be commenced on the 10th. On the 10th, the whole army would march in parallel columns to the neighborhood of Kingston, and on the 11th, to the neighborhood of Newbern. On the 12th, the battle would take place; and, as it is fought under particular circumstances, a few words of explanation are necessary.

The large concentration of troops, and the offensive operations immediately following, would result in a certain surprise of the Union army; and it is obvious that, in a fight so prepared, no time should be left to an enemy to recover from his surprise, and to take preparatory dispositions. The attack should therefore be executed in the same style as the whole offensive movement.

In the present case, there is another reason for a very energetic attack. The Union army is backed by a river; and in fact, its safety in such a position are its gun-boats, under the cover of which it is thought no disaster can happen to the troops. I am very far from sharing this opinion, and believe that whenever the attack is well prepared, and rightly executed, disaster must occur to an army so backed by a river, and protected only by gun-boats. Gun-boats are, after all, nothing but a few batteries of heavy guns, but batteries which are excessively vulnerable.

In European navies percussion shells, containing (besides the bursting charge) incendiary composition, are used against such wooden batteries. The shell is sure to burst within the ship, and the combustible matters are thrown in different directions; the smoke of the bursting shell preventing at first their discovery till it is too late. Those who wish to form an idea as to the effect of shells on ships, and especially those fired under such conditions, may read General Paixhans's memoirs on the matter, and the report of a commission of French officers to investigate the disaster of Sinope in 1854.

A few rifled 20-pounder batteries, firing such shells, and concentrating their fire successively on the different gun-boats, would soon drive them out of range; and if at this moment the attack against the land force is well prepared, by heavy masses of artillery drawing to very short canister range, and followed up by a general onset, disorder in the attacked party would ensue; and as no space to retreat and re-form is left, the slightest advantage gained becomes decisive, and finishes with the destruction of the whole, or at least of a great part, of an army placed in such a position. It may be said also that the attacking party should not give up the contest till the object—the destruction of the attacked force—is fully attained. It is evident that, whatever be the loss of the attack at the commencement, the defending party will at the end experience the greatest loss.

On the 13th, the day after the battle, the whole army leaves, with the exception of 10,000 men left on the battle-field to attend to the dead and wounded. The army moves to Kingston, and, on the 17th, is back at Weldon. From there, 35,000 are transported by railroad to Richmond, where they arrive between the 17th and 19th. The remaining 35,000 march to Suffolk, attack the Union forces there, and join the Richmond army on about the 25th to 27th of month 1. The 10,000 left on the battle-field may move by railroad to Charleston or Richmond; this movement depending on where the need of troops is the greatest. The general-in-chief leaves the army on the 13th to proceed to Chattanooga, where meanwhile another great movement has been prepared.

Evidently 87,000 men, or the number of the Virginia army after the deduction of 33,000 men for Goldsborough, would never be able to resist 140,000 men, which we have supposed to be the strength of the Potomac army. It would therefore be a great mistake to engage with this number in a battle. All that is required, is to observe the army of the Potomac, and when it moves forward to retard its march: 50,000 men are quite sufficient to accomplish this task, and even more fit for it than 87,000; because a smaller number can always be quicker put in motion, and if a disaster occurs, the risk is not so great.

We reduce, therefore, the army of Virginia by 27,000 men more, which we would send to Tennessee, giving positive orders to the remaining 50,000 to accept no engagement of consequence; to retreat if the army of the Potomac advances; and to be satisfied with defending the passage of the rivers, beating an advanced guard, etc.

The campaign in Tennessee, as the next in importance, we would conduct almost simultaneously with that against

Newbern; and this is possible in the present case: first, because the Union armies of Newbern and Murfreesborough are not large; and secondly, because the army sent to Goldsborough is not far from the decisive point, which we will suppose to be Richmond, and might be back there before a Union army could reach it.

It is evident that all the troops executing these different manœuvres are to be in the lightest marching order; and to facilitate their rapid movement, the inhabitants of the places through which troops pass ought to be instructed to prepare rations sufficient for the number of troops passing, for which they are to be liberally remunerated.

The movements against Murfreesborough might be combined in the following way:—

| | | |
|---|---|---|
| Army at Tullahoma | 50,000 | men. |
| From the army of Virginia | 27,000 | " |
| " " Vicksburg | 25,000 | " |
| " " Mobile | 5,000 | " |
| " different detachments, etc | 10,000 | " |
| Total | 117,000 | " |

The 25,000 men from Vicksburg ought to be partly replaced by the 15,000 from Arkansas and Texas.

The following table will show how the concentration is to be conducted—the different corps being transported all by railroad as far as Chattanooga and London. From this line as a base, the movement is to be executed. We suppose, as we have done before, that the longer railroad lines are able to transport 2500 men per diem; and that on some of the shorter, the number might be augmented by running the cars day and night, and by stopping for a few days all other traffic:—

| Men. | Start by railroad from— | For— | Month 1. | Arrive at— | Month 1. |
|---|---|---|---|---|---|
| 2500 each day.. | Fredericksburg.. | Lynchburg, Knoxville; Cleveland. | 4th and 5th.... | Cleveland..... | 5th and 6th. |
| 2500 " " | Fredericksburg.. | Lynchburg, Knoxville, Cleveland. | 6th and 7th.... | Cleveland..... | 7th and 8th. |
| 2500 " " | Fredericksburg.. | Lynchburg, Knoxville, Cleveland. | 8th and 9th.... | Cleveland..... | 9th and 10th. |
| 2500 " " | Fredericksburg.. | Lynchburg, Knoxville, Cleveland | 10th and 11th. | Cleveland..... | 11th and 12th. |
| 2500 " " | Fredericksburg.. | Lynchburg, Knoxville, Cleveland. | 12th and 13th. | Cleveland..... | 13th and 14th. |
| 2500=27,000... | Fredericksburg.. | Lynchburg, Knoxville, Cleveland. | 14th............ | Cleveland..... | 15th. |
| 5000............ | Vicksburg ....... | Mobile ................................ | 1st............... | Mobile......... | 1st. |
| 5000............ | Vicksburg ....... | Mobile ................................ | 2d ............... | Mobile......... | 2d. |
| 5000............ | Vicksburg ....... | Mobile ................................ | 3d ............... | Mobile......... | 3d. |
| 5000............ | Vicksburg ....... | Mobile ................................ | 4th............... | Mobile......... | 4th. |
| 5000=25,000... | Vicksburg ....... | Mobile ................................ | 5th............... | Mobile......... | 5th. |
| 2500 each day.. | Mobile ........... | Chattanooga ........................ | 2d and 3d...... | Chattanooga. | 4th and 5th. |
| 2500=10,000. | Mobile ........... | Chattanooga ........................ | 4th and 5th.... | Chattanooga. | 6th and 7th. |
| 2500 each day.. | Mobile ........... | Harrison ............................. | 6th and 7th.... | Harrison...... | 8th and 9th. |
| 2500 " " | Mobile ........... | Harrison ............................. | 8th and 9th.... | Harrison...... | 10th and 11th. |
| 2500 " " | Mobile ........... | Harrison ............................. | 10th and 11th. | Harrison...... | 12th and 13th. |
| 2500=20,000... | Mobile ........... | Harrison ............................. | 12th and 13th. | Harrison...... | 14th and 15th. |
| 7000 } 10,000... | Detachments, guerrillas, and cavalry from Kentucky (comprised in the table giving the respective forces)............ | | { 7000. | London........ | 12th. |
| 3000 } | | | { 3000. | Cleveland..... | 13th. |

On the 14th, the commander-in-chief should arrive at Chattanooga; and on the same day the offensive operation should be commenced. With 117,000 men against 40,000 to 50,000, a commander can well propose to himself to destroy this latter army; and the only correct way to do this is to execute similar manœuvres to those executed by Napoleon in 1805 and 1806,—the relative position of the base of operation of the Rebels to that of the line of operation of the Union army facilitating such action.

We will try to describe such a movement here, though the task is somewhat above our abilities, notwithstanding we have the brilliant examples of 1805 and 1806 before our eyes.

On the 13th of month 1st, 7000 men start from London, and march for Crossville. On the 15th of month 1st, 30,000 men start from Cleveland, on the road to Sparta, and cross the Tennessee.

For easier understanding, I have added an engraving, showing the position of the different corps. *U. S.* is the Union army, stationed nine to ten miles south from Murfreesborough. For better distinction, we will divide the Rebel army into divisions of 10,000, numbered from one to twelve, as shown on the plate. (See Fig. 8.)

On the 16th, all the divisions are put in motion. Division 6 starts from Chattanooga, and is on the 18th, in the evening, at Manchester; 7 and 8 march from Harrison for *R*, where they arrive on the 18th, in the evening; 9 and 10 leave Tennessee River, and arrive at McMinnsville on the 18th, in the evening; and finally, divisions 11 and 12 march,

Fig. 8.

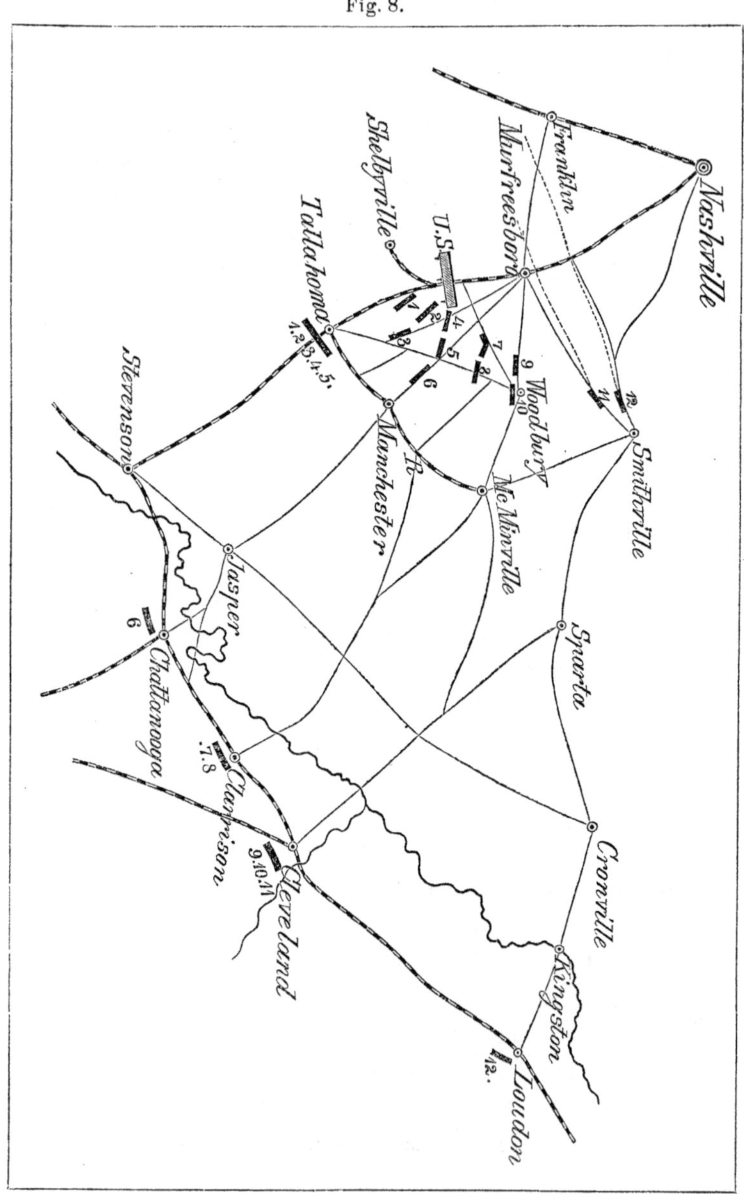


NOTE.—Read London for Loudon ; Crossville for Cronville; Harrison for Clarrison.

by way of Sparta, to about ten miles from Smithville, where they arrive also on the 18th, in the evening.

All distances, as will be seen, are three days' march. On the 19th, the divisions arrive in the positions shown in the engraving; and for the 20th, the action is impending. On the 20th, divisions 11 and 12 start on their respective routes at four o'clock A.M. At two o'clock, they have to strike the railroad above Murfreesborough; and at five o'clock, they have to be half way to Franklin, on the Franklin and Murfreesborough Turnpike. Division 12, which should consist in great part of cavalry, with some batteries, should be very near Franklin at that time.

On the same day, divisions 9 and 10 start at four o'clock A.M., and march for Murfreesborough, where they should be at twelve o'clock, changing their front, and moving in a southwesterly direction. (The map at my disposal is not exact enough to designate any special point.) These corps have to communicate with divisions 7 and 8, and may receive special orders about the direction they are to take during the day.

On the 20th, also in the morning, at five o'clock, 7 and 8 move against the railroad, half way between Murfreesborough and the Union army, from where they have to be at about nine o'clock; then they take also a southwesterly direction to join in the battle at about ten o'clock, and to attack the extreme right and rear of the Union army.

Finally, divisions 1, 2, 3, 4, 5, and 6 attack the Union army *U. S.* at six o'clock in the morning, holding at first somewhat back till 7 and 8 arrive on the battle-field, when the reserves are brought in the action and the *coup-de-collier* is given. Should the retreat of the U. S. troops commence very early, and in the direction of Franklin, the direction of 9, 10, 11, and 12 should be changed to clear west, or perhaps even somewhat west-northwest. These corps have to pursue on the flank of the Union army, and continually prevent its going north; the remainder of the Rebel army pursue in the rear. A few days of such pursuit, especially if the battle has been conducted with great energy, would entirely break up and finish the U. S. army, the remainder of which would, besides, be obliged to surrender near the Tennessee River.

The great mistake to be avoided in the battle, is one similar to that committed by Ney in the battle of Bautzen. The corps 7, 8, 9, and 10 have always to act more to their right than to their left; and wherever they meet the enemy, they have to attack with the utmost impetuosity, and to fall headlong on him. The reason for such action is obvious. By the direction of their march, they will appear in the flank or rear of an army already fully engaged in front against superior numbers. To proceed slowly under such circumstances, would give the attacked army time to retreat and escape from the impending peril.

After the battle, 117,000 men are obviously too many to pursue some 25,000 or 30,000 constituting the remainder of the Union army. Under these circumstances, a division of force is according to the rules; therefore, immediately after the battle, the divisions 3, 5, and 6 march to Nashville, which town they attack on the 21st, in the afternoon, and which they have to carry by assault. These three divisions ought to be well provided with artillery for this purpose. After the capture of Nashville, the divisions 3, 5, and 6 cross the Cumberland and march to Gallatin. On the 25th they ought to be at Glasgow, Kentucky; 27th at Mumfordsville, beating and destroying all smaller Union corps on their way. On the 27th they might be at Lebanon, and, if there is the slightest chance of the capture of Louisville, it should be attempted; after which the movement is to be continued to Lexington, pushing cavalry parties as far as Covington. From Lexington the corps proceed to Cumberland Gap, and arrive at Rodgersville Junction about the 20th of month 2. From there they will be transported by rail to the East, so as to form a junction with the Rebel armies in the left zone. This junction ought to be effected by the 1st of month 3.

The main army, some 80,000 strong, is meanwhile marching by forced marches toward Savannah, Tenn., or any point where the pursuit of the Cumberland army carries it to, or where it can easily cross the Tennessee River. Supposing that the crossing will take place at Savannah, where the army has arrived on the 26th of month 1, on the 27th the crossing and advance to Purdy takes place; on the 28th 15,000 men march to Jackson, the same day 35,000 more to Bolivar, 20,000 to Pocahontas, and 10,000 remain on the road from Purdy to Corinth. On the 29th the Union troops at Bolivar and Jackson are beaten; those at the former place are pursued by 15,000, and those at the latter by 3000 or 4000, of which about 2000 should be cavalry, and which troops should push on as far as Columbus. The remaining 10,000 or 12,000 march to Somerville or Raleigh, and form, on the 2d of month 2, a junction with the 15,000 Rebel troops coming from Bolivar. An attack on Memphis should take place immediately, if this place has not meanwhile been reinforced by Union troops returning from Vicksburg. The remainder of the 35,000 at Bolivar march to Pocahontas, join with the 20,000 there, and proceed on the 30th to the attack of Corinth, which, attacked by 50,000 men, and from several sides, would be obliged to surrender. After this action, the Rebel troops should have two or three days of repose, and then commence their eastward movement. The troops left before Memphis, after the capture of this place, should also commence their movement to the East. By using all possible means, as far as railroads are concerned, this whole army ought to be, by the 1st of month 3, in the left zone, ready to effect a junction with the Rebel forces there. The beating of the armies at Corinth, Bolivar, Memphis, etc. necessarily disengages Vicksburg, if this place has not meanwhile been carried by the Union troops. We have supposed that the Rebel troops there have been reinforced by 15,000 troops from Arkansas. If those 40,000 have been able to withstand all assaults undertaken by the Federal army, it cannot be doubted that about the 2d or 3d of month 2 the siege of Vicksburg would be raised. This should immediately be taken advantage of by sending 30,000 men to the East, where they should arrive also about the 1st of month 3. By using the Mobile and Savannah and Lynchburg and Knoxville Roads, 5000 troops ought to be conveyed daily from west to east.

We have now to return to the East, to see what has happened meanwhile there.

Probably, after some time, the departure of so great a number of troops from the Virginia army for the South and West will be noticed by the army of the Potomac, and a forward movement will take place. Three directions may be chosen by this army for its advance toward Richmond, the capture of which we still suppose to be the object of its offensive campaign. These three directions are given strategically in the action of the center, by the right or by the left. The action by the center means a straight movement from Fredericksburg toward Richmond, taking the road leading from the first to the latter place as the line of operation. The crossing of the Rappahannock would be required in this case, and this crossing, simply considered as a tactical operation, might take place just as the whole operation, considered strategically, would, viz., by the right, left, or center; that is to say, the army may cross some miles above Fredericksburgh, turning thereby the left of the Rebel army and marching straight to Bowling Green or Sexton Station; or it may cross below, and turn the right of the Rebel army by marching to Bowling Green; or, finally, it may cross at Fredericksburg, and attack the Rebels in front. This latter expedient has already been tried in the battle of Fredericksburg, and it failed; however, considering the weakened state of the Rebel army, it might be tried again. This latter army, as we have seen, after sending 30,000 men to Newbern, sends 27,000 off to Richmond, which place they leave by lots of 2500 for the West, the last lot starting on the 14th of month 1. Immediately after the departure of these corps, the Rebel army takes the following position: 20,000 remain in and near Fredericksburg, 5000 march to Chancellorsville, and stay there, and finally 25,000 move to Bowling Green, to await events. The Rappahannock is strongly picketed from Fredericksburg some 10 or 15 miles above and below, to prevent any surprise. Should the Union army cross once more to Fredericksburg, the 20,000 men there would be joined, within three or four hours, by the 5000 at Chancellorsville and the 25,000 at Bowling Green; and, as at the first battle of Fredericksburg scarcely more than 50,000 Rebels were actually engaged, it might be that the remaining 50,000 would be able to repulse the attack, or at all events to inflict serious loss. It would probably take till night before their position was carried, and then they would have time to retreat, and place the Mattapony between them and their pursuers. The bridges over this river would be destroyed, and another river defense would take place; the same game would be repeated at North and South Anna River, at the Chickahominy, and at Little River; till, finally, arrived near Richmond, the Rebel army takes shelter under the cannon of the fortifications of their capital.

Should the Union army cross below Fredericksburg, and advance straight to Bowling Green, the 25,000 Rebels at this place would cross the Mattapony, destroy the bridges, and defend the passage over the river, till joined by the remainder of the Rebel force from Fredericksburg and Chancellorsville, who would have marched by forced marches, and by way of Mount Pleasant, to a junction with their friends.

The fight at Fredericksburg would therefore be avoided, but at the Mattapony the same difficulties in crossing would be experienced as before. Evidently the Mattapony, as well as all the subsequent rivers, may be crossed above or below the defending forces, who would have to conduct the defenses entirely according to the rules laid down for such operations. (See "Summary of the Art of War.") Finally, should the Union army cross above Fredericksburg, it would immediately be attacked by the 5000 at Chancellorsville and 20,000 at Fredericksburg, who would soon be joined by the 25,000 from Bowling Green. Once the passage effected, the case is the same as the two preceding. The Union army advances, and the Rebel army retreats in the direction of Richmond and along the Fredericksburg and Richmond Railroad.

Let us suppose the movement of the Federal army to be commenced on the 5th of month 1. Considering the difficulties of the advance, the crossing of five or six rivers over which bridges have to be built, and, finally, the necessity for rebuilding the railroad bridges also, in order to use the railroad for supplying the army,—considering all this, we could not suppose that the army would take less than 10 to 12 days to reach Richmond; it would probably take twice that time. Let us take 12 days, and say that on the 17th of month 1 the Federal troops find themselves in face of the Rebel capital, occupied at that time by some 60,000 to 65,000 men—50,000 from Fredericksburg, 5000 who were left as garrison, and some 5000 to 10,000 men who have had time to arrive after the battle of Newbern.

Richmond being fortified, two ways of action are open for its capture—either a general assault immediately after the arrival of the army, or the formal siege of the place. The fortifications around Richmond having more or less the character of field-works, a daring commander might try the assault. Field-works of such a description, defended by 65,000 men, who would be reinforced on the day of battle by some 20,000 more transported from Weldon and Petersburg, are difficult to take. The position would have to be carried without reference to the loss of life. The most energetic and decided action alone could warrant such an attempt or render it successful. To make an assault just to try the thing, at the same time being afraid of the loss, would evidently be useless—it would be repulsed with great carnage. Supposing the first kind of action—that is to say, decided action, like that of Napoleon at the battle of Smolensk or Borodino—to take place, it is necessary to consider the respective chances. The Union army arriving before Richmond would probably not amount to more than 100,000 to 110,000 men, as it would have to detach largely to cover its long line of communications with its bridges, etc. The Rebels would oppose them with 65,000 to 85,000 men, covered by redoubts and a strong artillery. The beating of these 85,000 men is not impossible under such circumstances; but if well led, they ought to be victorious in the end, and the loss of the attacking party after the repulse, considering the desperate nature of the attack, would be so enormous that it would probably force them to retreat. The more prudent course would, therefore, seem to be to undertake the siege; but whether it be so or not, we will suppose it to be undertaken without a previous assault.

The siege of Richmond would take a month at the least, perhaps two. Meantime the army must be supplied; it must therefore have a safe base and a secure line of communication. The most natural lines of communication that present themselves are the Fredericksburg and Richmond Railway line, the York River, York River Railroad, and the James River. The adoption of the two latter would force the army to a change of front, in order to protect its communications; but as these two cases are identical with the action of the Potomac army at Falmouth to its left, we will treat of them when speaking of the latter case. We therefore suppose, first, that the Federal army before Richmond keeps the Aquia Creek and Richmond Railway line as a line of communication, in order to obtain its supplies, etc. This line evidently requires strong detachments to protect it from surprise: 20,000 to 25,000 men, if not more, would certainly be necessary to guard the many bridges, the long trains of stores, and the temporary magazines at Aquia Creek and Fredericksburg, etc. On the 20th of month 1 the army in Richmond would be increased to 90,000, and a few days later to 125,000 men, by the arrival of 35,000 more, consisting of the corps which has marched against Suffolk and beaten the Federal army there. The Confederate forces would now be strong enough to take the offensive; but, in this case, temporizing would probably prove an advantage to them: first, because within a month they would be so heavily reinforced from the West that a decisive result, finishing the war, might be obtained; and secondly, the long line of operation of the Union forces would offer an excellent chance for beating them in detail, and hold out too great a temptation for a Jackson and a Stuart, united, to gather fresh laurels by capturing or destroying those Federal corps scattered over a long space of from 55 to 60 miles.

In order to execute such a raid, Jackson, with some 30,000 of good infantry, and Stuart, with some 4000 to 5000 cavalry, would move to Goochland C. H., and cross the James River there; thence they would march to Sexton's Junction, leaving a thousand cavalry, with about four guns, at South Ann River, in the neighborhood of Allen's Creek, for the purpose of informing the main body of any movement taking place in the Federal army, and for retarding the march of a corps which might be sent by the Federal commander toward Orange C. H. to intercept the Rebels in their retreat.

The main body, under Jackson and Stuart, arrived at a distance of about eight miles from Sexton's Junction, would detach some 12,000 infantry and 2000 cavalry to attack the Union post at South Ann River, provided this post does not number more than 4000 or 5000. If it should number more, it would be preferable to march there with the whole force, crush it, and destroy the bridges over the river; for it must be borne in mind that this post might be reinforced within an hour from the army before Richmond.

The next move is to North Ann River, then to the Mattapony and to the Rappahannock. The Union troops at

Fredericksburg are attacked, the bridges over the river destroyed, and the river itself passed above, and the movement continued to Aquia Creek. This whole movement must evidently be executed with great speed. Rapidity, energy, and determination would probably render it a complete success. The consequent retreat from Aquia Creek would depend entirely upon the action of the army of the Potomac. Three principal directions present themselves: a movement to Gordonsville, or to Culpepper, or to Warrenton and Thoroughfare Gap. The two latter would only be executed in order to reach the Shenandoah valley, and with it safety.

The Potomac army finds itself, in consequence of this raid, in an embarrassing situation. The Rebels would probably have spread reports of having 50,000 to 60,000 men with them in this raid; besides, the day the attack on South Ann River takes place, the army in Richmond would engage in a fight which would detain the Union forces, and prevent a large detachment being sent away. It must also be considered that the Federal army would probably number not more than 100,000 men; that to detach 40,000, 50,000, or 60,000, would leave only about 50,000 exposed to the blows of the 90,000 forming the defending army of Richmond, which, by crossing a few miles above Richmond, might attack the remainder of the Union army in flank, and destroy it before the detachment could return. Sending only a small detachment would expose the latter to a defeat by Jackson; besides, sending troops after the Rebels on the Richmond and Fredericksburg line would be entirely useless, as they would continually come too late. The only thing they would gain would be the latest reports of the depredations committed by the Rebels.

In a case like this, the real character of different generals would show itself. A Napoleon or a Cesar would, at the first notice of the raid, leave their trains and parks, and move with their whole army, by forced marches, toward Orange C. H. or Potteisville, according to circumstances. Executed against them, this raid would be destruction to the corps who undertook it. A Wellington would probably at first do nothing at all, but raise the siege as soon as the reports were fully confirmed, and move with his whole material composedly back to his first base. A Jourdan or a Victor would send a detachment after the Rebels, staying themselves with the main body before Richmond. A Moreau or Massena would get their trains in readiness, leave a strong detachment to cover them, with orders to retreat as soon as the Rebels in Richmond manifest a desire to attack, and with their main body they would march to intercept the Rebel corps which has undertaken the raid.

In our case, I think that the undertaking of the raid would be sufficiently justified by the simple fact that a Napoleon or Cesar would probably not have chosen the line of operation from Fredericksburg to Richmond.

It would occupy us too long to enter upon a discussion of how to act in a case like this. We may merely say that Jackson should by all means try to escape to the Shenandoah valley, and the Union forces should endeavor to prevent him from doing so. Once plunged in this valley, all pursuit would be useless, as the different gaps give him the facilities to execute movements similar to those of some Spanish generals—La Romana, for instance, in the Asturias and Gallicia, against Ney, where the latter descended one valley in pursuit of a Spanish column, which remounted at the same moment a parallel valley, separated from the first by impassable ridges, and thereby escaped.

If the siege, notwithstanding this raid, should be continued—the Rebels carrying on all the while a kind of counter-siege—the Confederate forces would have to prepare for a final and decisive action. In the middle and at the end of month 2, their reinforcements from the West begin to arrive; and by the 25th their strength is sufficient to allow of its coming to decisive blows. With the superiority they would have at that time, they should prepare themselves for more than simply beating the Union army; they should try to destroy it. The necessary movement for this might be executed in the following manner:—

About 200,000 troops are to be disposed along the Richmond and Burkesville Railroad, at Mattoax, Powhatan, Tomahawk, and Coal Mines. From there they advance, in one day, to Tay, and cross the James River; moving then, in the mode we have indicated for the engagement in Tennessee, by parallel columns, the right wing to Hungary, pushing a detachment to Scuffletown, the center on the road from Montpellier to Richmond, and the left wing at Ashland. After having taken possession of all the bridges over the Chickahominy, the army changes front to the south. The advanced guard of the center becomes the left wing, and the reserve which marched with the center becomes the center, the left becomes the reserve.

The Union army is attacked in this way in its rear by some 180,000 or 200,000 men. Moreover, 40,000 or 50,000 debouch from Richmond and attack its left, to prevent its retreating once more to Harrison's Landing or Malvern Hill. If, under such circumstances, the battle is rightly planned and carried out with sufficient speed, it must end with the entire destruction of the Federal army, which is inclosed between the fortifications of Richmond and the main Rebel army, and has, besides, a corps of 50,000 men on its flank. After this battle, the Rebels have to take the offensive against the North. We will treat of this hereafter.

The Union army, instead of acting by the center, may act by its left—that is, for its advance from Fredericksburg it may cross the Rappahannock very far below, at Urbana, for instance, march to York River, cross it by means of steamers, and push toward Richmond from West Point or White House as a base. Or it may be transported to James River, taking this river as a base, and move either on its right or its left bank toward Richmond. The distinctive feature of this manœuvre by the left is, that the army would base itself on a river, and the navy would have to play a great part in the operations. The cases to be considered, as we have already seen, are three: 1, York River as a base; 2, James River as a base, with an advance on the right bank against Richmond; 3, James River as a base, with an advance on the left bank against Richmond.

Taking York River as a base, the Union army would have to go over the campaign on the Chickahominy once more. It could not be supposed that the Rebel army would be surprised, or their corps at Fredericksburg be outflanked by the movement of the Federal troops to West Point, as they might reach Richmond in two days from Fredericksburg, the distance being only some 60 miles. If General Banks's soldiers in the Shenandoah valley could march 60 miles in two days, those of Jackson or Longstreet might well travel the same distance in the same time. Considering carefully such a movement, consisting partly of transportation, partly of marching, it would be found that in less than 10 or 12 days the Union army, leaving Fredericksburg, could scarcely reach Richmond. It would arrive there without previous loss, and this certainly is to be taken into account. It is not necessary to discuss the chances of the campaign against the Confederate capital, with York River as a base. The study of the campaign of the Potomac army in 1862 will be sufficient to show the dangers and difficulties an army would have to contend with.

Choosing James River as a base of operation against Richmond, the army might reach there by marching from York River to Harrison's Landing or Malvern Hill, or any other place on this river where the army would be in communication with the gun-boats and transports; or the army might arrive at the appointed place by being transported to it from Aquia Creek. This arrangement would evidently take a great length of time, and in no case could the army be before or near Richmond under 12 to 15 days, counted from its starting from Fredericksburg. Arrived at James River, let us suppose, first, that the advance takes place on the right bank of this river. If so, much will depend if Petersburg and Walthall form fortified double *têtes-de-pont*, able to resist an attack of a strong army; much also depends on Fort Darling forming a similar fortified double *tête-de-pont*. Should, in fact, a system of fortifications exist such as we have spoken of in Chapter III., Fig. 5, little can be expected from the action of the Federal army. It would, in order to approach Richmond, have to make the siege of Petersburg, and especially of Fort Darling, in the first instance, and this in the face of an army of 120,000 men, which within a month would be reinforced by 125,000 men more. The Union army might think itself lucky if, after some attempts to carry the fortifications, it could save one-half of its numbers; and certainly the Rebels would deserve severe criticism if so large a portion of the Union army should escape, inclosed as it is or would be by the James and Appomattox Rivers, and by a Rebel army acting against its left flank and its rear.

If no fortifications exist at Petersburg and Walthall, if, moreover, the James River is open to gun-boats and transports above Appomattox River, then the Union army might at once cross above this latter river and advance against Manchester. The gun-boats could only follow as far as Fort Darling, and if the Union army would advance farther, it would run straight into destruction. Evidently the Rebel army would not commit so ridiculous a blunder as to place itself square before Manchester. It would take a position at Coal Mines or Tomahawk, on the left flank of the Union army, and, as soon as the latter would have advanced above Fort Darling, it would immediately advance to Cedar Row, taking the Federals on the left flank and rear, and throwing them into the corner formed by the James River at Richmond or Manchester. Should the Union army be defeated in such a battle, its total loss would evidently be the consequence. To avoid such a disaster, the reduction of Fort Darling and the opening of James River would probably be tried before any farther advance against Richmond takes place. This, however, the Rebels should endeavor to prevent by all means. They should attack the left flank of the Union army with impetuosity; they should construct in the James River other bars above the first; should drive off the gun-boats by firing incendiary shells at them; they should continually reinforce, till their superiority had become such that the Union army could not resist a further assault, and is finally thrown into the river. Here, as well as before, if the attack is executed rightly, the Federal army ought, in consequence of its position, backed by a river, to be completely destroyed, and the gun-boats should not be able to save it. In this operation—that is, along the right bank of the James River—the Federal army is obviously more exposed than in our first operation, when acting along the railroad from Fredericksburg. Its entire safety depends on its gun-boats; it has no space to manœuvre in, to advance, or to retreat; it is chained to James River, and the slightest accident happening to the flotilla, the appearance and fortunate action of a Merrimac No. 2, for instance, would be the ruin of this army.

There remains to be considered the advance against Richmond along the left bank of James River, from a point below Fort Darling as a base. An attack on this side would lead to the same disasters as on the right bank, if the crossings over the Chickahominy remained in possession of the Rebels. Holding the bridges over this creek, the Rebels might at any moment debouch against the right flank of the Union army, and throw it against the James River; or, if Fort Darling forms a double *tête-de-pont,* they might cross the James River there, and attack the Union army in the rear. This fort, if forming a *tête-de-pont,* ought, therefore, to be masked or reduced before the Federal army proceeds any farther. This takes time, and meanwhile the Rebel army is continually reinforced; the final result can, therefore, not be doubtful. No special manœuvre could be made by the Rebel troops when once the siege was commenced, unless by holding the bridges over the Chickahominy from Meadow to Bottom Bridge, and, passing behind the creek, they were to debouch by these bridges and attack the Union army in the rear. It would be a manœuvre somewhat similar to that of 1862, executed on the same spot. If this manœuvre is impossible, mere strength or numbers would decide; only tactically the attack would probably be directed against the center or right wing of the Union forces, as in both these cases, if the attack is successful, great results would be obtained.

We have, lastly, to consider the third case, that of the Union army acting by its right. This operation differs from the two others only by the route the army takes. Once before Richmond, in order to make the siege, one of the four cases already considered will take place, as the army, for its supplies, has to base itself on Aquia Creek or York or James River. (If Richmond were not fortified, the operation to the right would be decisive.) We have supposed, in our imaginary campaign, that only 50,000 men oppose the army of the Potomac; these have, therefore, nothing better to do, when the Union army commences its movement to the right, than to march, at first parallel with the Federal army, and then retreat to Richmond. The defense of rivers is out of question, as the Union army may pass high enough, where the rivers are so unimportant that their defense would be of no avail. Little would, therefore, be changed by this action to the right, and only the fights on the different crossings avoided. Were the Rebel army equal, or very nearly so, to the Federal army, the matter would be different. In the same way that the Union army moves to the right the Rebels should move to their left, continually parallel with the Union army, and finally, arrived near Gordonsville, they might, by making good use of the different gaps, perhaps be able to beat the Union army in detail. At all events, here the Confederates might permit the Union forces to pass to their right and to march toward Richmond, provided that place has a sufficient garrison, and, by following this army immediately, render its march a kind of retreat. Should the Federals, under such circumstances, try an assault against Richmond, their rear and right flank would be attacked at the same moment by the entire Rebel army, the case being the same as the one we first considered, viz., the Union army undertaking the siege of Richmond, having Aquia Creek as a base.

Returning to our imaginary campaign, it will be understood that, immediately after the decisive defeat of the Union army before Richmond, the offensive should be taken against the North. If the destruction has been complete, the entire Rebel army should move. If the defeat has been only such as after the seven days' fight, 50,000 men left at Richmond would be sufficient to defend the town; the remainder—some 180,000 to 200,000—should move on the day after the battle, by forced marches, to the North. Washington we will suppose strongly garrisoned, as well as Harper's Ferry and Baltimore. At Warrenton 30,000 men would be detached, to move by way of Centreville against the Federal capital, as a kind of corps of observation: 20,000 men would be sent through Ashby's Gap against Winchester, and thence against Martinsburg. Arrived at Buckletown, they would march east, and thereby prevent the garrison of Harper's Ferry escaping west or northwest. The main body of the army has meanwhile moved along Loudon valley; at Aldie Gap about 100,000 pass through it; the remainder (some 40,000) move to Berlin; a detachment takes Loudon Heights; 10,000 men move to Frederick-town, and the remaining 30,000 march into Pleasant Valley, take Maryland Heights, and force the garrison of Harper's Ferry once more to surrender. Immediately after the surrender, and if in the meanwhile Washington has been captured, the entire corps moves toward Chambersburg, for an invasion of the North; if Washington has not been captured, then it moves against Baltimore. The main body having passed through Aldie Gap, advances to Con's Ferry, crosses the Potomac, and immediately proceeds toward Washington, which place ought to be attacked simultaneously, on the right bank of the Potomac by the 30,000 Rebels coming from Centreville, and by the 100,000 coming from Con's Ferry on the left bank. One or two forts carried on the left bank would open the way into the city, and this once occupied, the garrison in the forts on the right would probably be obliged to surrender.

This short exposé will show that the Rebels, by taking to grand offensive operations under the present circumstances; by defeating first the smaller Union bodies, and then by concentrating all their forces for the last decisive struggle; by leaving the Union armies in the West, far away from the decisive point, perfectly free to capture cotton plantations, and open Western rivers to Northern navigation, while they (the Rebels) are dealing decisive blows, and capturing large Union cities in the East, might finish the war to their own advantage, and this simply in consequence of the wrong plan of conquest followed by the Northern troops.

Grand operations, however, as we have just described them, demand for their execution more than ordinary talents in the leader; and the question would be, have the Confederates a general able to execute such movements and manœuvres? Supposing they have not, and supposing they keep strictly on the defensive, (which, in their case, is obviously a mistake,) and that the defense is conducted according to the rules of military science, even then they might protract the war, and perhaps prevent any decisive result being obtained by the North.

The whole course of our imaginary campaign was based on two preliminary successes—the destruction of the Cumberland and the Newbern armies. If once those gaps were made in the immense front of operation of the Union armies, the remainder of this front must break to pieces. In a purely defensive campaign, the Rebels would be satisfied with repulsing the Union armies, instead of destroying them.

The army of the Potomac, in its advance, would have to contend with exactly the same difficulties, and perhaps even with more, if the Virginia army should not have been weakened by strong detachments, as we have supposed in our imaginary campaign. Arrived before Richmond, the same difficulties about the line of communication and base of operation, that we have discussed, would occur. The Rebels, receiving a few reinforcements from Tennessee, Vicksburg, and Charleston, would be able to take the offensive. Acting according to the position of the Union army, as we have shown above, the final retreat of the army of the Potomac can scarcely be doubted, if the defense is anything like correctly and vigorously conducted. As soon as the Potomac army retreats, the Rebels would send reinforcements to the West, to push back the Union armies which have meanwhile advanced.

The army of the Cumberland, after the bloody battle of Murfreesborough, might advance. It finds its enemy in line of battle at Tullahoma. Another victory and another advance only find the enemy once more in line of battle behind the Tennessee. A third victory, and General Rosecrans might find himself in the situation of Pyrrhus, when, after his victory over the Romans, he said, "*One more victory like this, and I am undone.*"

The armies of the Mississippi may take Vicksburg; but what is gained, what is achieved if they do? Another post which must be occupied by Union troops; a blessing for the Rebels, who obtain by it some 40,000 or 50,000 men free for action elsewhere. But, by opening the Mississippi, the whole right zone will be separated from the rest of the theater of war. The Rebels cannot draw thence any more reinforcements and provisions, and we have often been told that the rebellion, in that case, is bound to fall. This assertion, before being credited, requires proof. It is but an assertion. The capture of Vicksburg would give the Rebels some 40,000 to 50,000 men, who might immediately be brought to the Tennessee to join the Rebel army there, and defeat the Cumberland army. The Mississippi Union armies would perhaps advance into the State of Mississippi; this would be another chance for the two united Rebel armies to gain a victory.

The army at Newbern, what can it achieve besides some annoyance to the Rebels? March to Raleigh? This might prove disastrous, at least it ought to do so; and even if it does not, after awhile the Union army would be obliged to retreat. Capture Wilmington? Be it so; but what would be gained by taking this town, beyond the necessity of sending another detachment to hold it? The conquest of the South is not one inch advanced by it.

Finally, let us suppose Richmond carried, Raleigh taken, Charleston occupied, Chattanooga seized, and the Union armies from the West advanced to the Tombigbee River; but the Rebel armies still existing, and still holding their interior lines, which become the more valuable and the more effective the more the Union armies approach, what prevents them from uniting all their forces nearly in one, gaining thereby a decisive superiority over every one of the surrounding Federal armies, defeating the Cumberland army first, the Newbern army next, and the army of the Potomac last, and regaining in a few weeks all they have lost the last few months?

It is like the work of Penelope, done by day and undone by night; only with this difference, that we do it in the spring, and the Rebels undo it in the fall.

In war sometimes accidents happen, accidents above human power to prevent; they are like the interfering of Providence. Napoleon, after the battle of Dresden, was the victim of one of these accidents. The Allies had crowned all the blunders they had committed before and in the battle of Dresden, in 1813, by a retreat against all military rules and even against all common sense. The destruction of nearly half their army would have been the consequence, had Napoleon not been taken ill by a violent attack of fever, compelling him to go home after the battle. The pursuit was badly conducted, and not only obtained no advantageous results, but ended even in the disaster of Culm, where nearly an entire corps of Napoleon's army was destroyed. It is difficult to say what turn events would have